A Simple Story

LEILA
GUERRIERO

translated by Thomas Bunstead

PUSHKIN PRESS
LONDON

Pushkin Press
71–75 Shelton Street
London WC2H 9JQ

Work published within the framework of "Sur" Translation Support
Program of the Ministry of Foreign Affairs and Worship of the Argentine
Republic.

Obra editada en el marco del Programa "Sur" de Apoyo a las Traducciones
del Ministerio de Relaciones Exteriores y Culto de la República Argentina.

A Simple Story was first published in Spanish as
Una historia sencilla

First published by Pushkin Press in 2015

0 0 1

ISBN 978 1 782271 59 8

Text designed and typeset by Tetragon, London

Printed by CPI Group (UK) Ltd, Croydon, CRO 4YY

www.pushkinpress.com

THIS IS THE STORY of a man who took part in a dance contest.

———————————

LABORDE, A TOWN three hundred miles north-west of Buenos Aires in Argentina's Córdoba province, was founded in 1903, originally under the name Las Liebres. Populated at the time by Italian immigrants, it now has six thousand inhabitants and is situated in an oasis of wheat and corn dotted with mills. The wheat and corn brought a reasonable level of prosperity to the area, nowadays maintained by soya cultivation, that manifests in towns that seem straight out of the mind of a very orderly, or perhaps psychotic, child: each of the compact town centres features a church, a main square, a town hall, and houses each with their own front garden and the latest gleaming Toyota 4 × 4, sometimes two, parked outside. Route 11 passes through a large number of such towns, places like Monte Maíz, Escalante, Pascanas. Laborde lies between Escalante and Pascanas – church, town square, town hall, houses with front gardens, 4 × 4, et cetera; a town like many others, in an agricultural area like many others; one of thousands of places in the country's vast interior whose name would ring no bells for most Argentinians. But, for certain people with a very specific interest, Laborde is an important place. In fact, for these people – with this specific interest – there is no place in the world more important than Laborde.

———————————

ON MONDAY, 5th January 2009, the Argentinian daily *La Nación* ran an article in its arts supplement, written by the journalist Gabriel Plaza, with the headline: 'The folk athletes line up'. Comprising two small columns on the front page and two medium-sized columns a couple of pages in, it included the following lines: "Considered an elite corps within the world of traditional folk dance, past champions, on the streets of Laborde at least, are treated with all the respect of ancient Greek sporting legends." I hung on to the article – weeks, months, and it was still in my thoughts – and then I found that years had elapsed, and still I was thinking about it. I'd never heard of Laborde before, but once I'd read this piece of red-hot information, the joining together of *elite corps* and *sporting legends* with *traditional dance* and *a town in the middle of nowhere*... I couldn't stop thinking. What about? About going and seeing, I suppose.

———————————

GAUCHO, according to the *Dictionary of Argentinian Folklore* (edited by Félix Coluccio and Susana Coluccio), is "the word used in the Río Plata region – Argentina and Uruguay – to designate the cowboys of these prairie- or pampas-lands... Cowboys and hired hands, by and large, they stood out for their physical prowess, as well as their haughty, reserved and melancholic manner. Almost all their tasks were carried out from the back of a horse, making the animal their best companion, and crucial to the wealth of the gaucho." The general, perhaps prejudiced view of the gaucho confers very particular characteristics: brave, loyal, strong, indomitable and austere, he is also reserved and arrogant, as well as being prone to the solitary, nomadic life.

As for malambo, in the words of the nineteenth-century folklorist Ventura Lynch, it consists of "a joust between men who take turns to dance to music". A dance the gauchos would challenge one another with, trying to best their opponents in feats of stamina and skill, to the accompaniment of a guitar and a drum. This is the dance Gabriel Plaza's article was alluding to: malambo, the dance of the gauchos.

_____

MALAMBO'S ORIGINS are unclear, though people agree it probably arrived in Argentina from Peru. Sets of tap dance-like movements, each associated with a certain musical metre, combine to form the "figures". Composed of taps of the toes, soles and heels, pauses on the balls of the feet, and lifts and twists – unimaginable contortions – of the ankles, a malambo performance at the highest level will include more than twenty such figures, divided up by *repiqueteos* – toe taps at a pace of no fewer than eight per second – requiring enormous responsiveness in the muscles. Each side has to be mirrored, a right-foot figure immediately repeated, identically, with the left foot, so that a dancer of malambo needs equal precision, strength, speed and elegance on both sides. There are two styles: *sureño* – hailing from Argentina's southern and central provinces – and *norteño* – from the north. *Sureño* is the gentler style, and is accompanied by just the guitar; *norteño* is more explosive, and calls for both a guitar and a drum. Dancers of each also dress differently: the southern- and central-province dancers wearing a wide-brimmed hat, a white shirt, neckerchief, waistcoat, short jacket, and the *cribo* – white, flared trousers with tassels and embroidery – over the top of which comes a kneelength section of fabric, somewhat like a skirt, known as the *chiripá*; a linen cord holds the *chiripá* up, but a wide, silver-decked belt (known as a *rastra*) is also worn; on the feet, the so-called "foal shoes", thin leather bindings covering only the heels and middle section of the foot, are tied on with rawhide straps that go over the ankles and around the calves – leaving the front part of the foot and toes bare as they strike the boards. The *norteño* style includes shirt, a cloth at the neck, jacket, *bombachas* – flowing, pleated trousers – and knee-high leather boots.

This strictly masculine dance, which began life as a crude kind of gauntlet-throwing, had by the twentieth century been strictly choreographed into performances lasting between two and five minutes. Though best known for the versions seen in "for export" spectacles – including hopscotch between candles and the juggling of knives – some traditional festivals in the country do still cleave close to malambo's essence. But it is in Laborde, this town out in the middle of pampas flatlands, where malambo in its purest form is preserved: since 1966 a prestigious and formidable six-day competition has been held here, one that places fierce physical demands on the participants and concludes with a winner who, not unlike bulls or other thoroughbred animals, is given the title of Champion.

IN 1966, on the initiative of an association calling itself Amigos de Arte, the Laborde National Malambo Competition was first held, in the grounds of a local sports club. In 1973 the organizing committee – locals who, as they do to this day, counted among their number manicurists and speech therapists, schoolteachers and small business owners, bakers and housewives – bought a thousand square metre plot of land from the local Spanish Association, and constructed a stage there. A crowd of two thousand people came that year. Nowadays over six thousand regularly attend, and, though the emphasis remains firmly on the malambo, the competition categories now include song, such as the Best Solo Recital category; music, such as Best Instrumental Ensemble; and other traditional dances, including Twosomes and Most Authentic Regional Presentation. Some of the best-attended slots feature non-competitive presentations from renowned musicians and folk-singing groups like Chango Spasiuk, Peteco Carabajal and La Callejera. Each year, dancers come in from across Argentina, but also farther afield – Bolivia, Chile and Paraguay in particular – swelling the town's numbers by an extra two thousand. Many locals rent out their homes, and the municipal schools become overflowing temporary hostels. Months of planning go into deciding who will participate, with delegations from each of Argentina's provinces pre-selecting the best dancers from their respective federations.

The organizing committee is self-financing, and refuses to have anything to do with the country's large traditional dance festivals (those held in Cosquín and Jesús María), veritable tsunamis of tradition that get broadcast nationwide. That would mean making the festival gaudy, trashy, and neither the running time (7 p.m. to 6 a.m.), nor the content itself, are what one could call easily digestible; you won't find pomaded gauchos wearing nice suits or tap-dancing between candles, and you won't find any rhinestone boots. If Laborde calls itself "the most Argentine festival" it's because it offers up *"tradición pura y dura"* – tradition, pure and hard. The regulations prohibit anything cutting-edge, and the jury, comprising former champions and folk dance specialists, wants to see folkloric tradition, as the regulations say, "without the remix": costumes and footwear that show respect for the modesty, or indeed the opulence, associated with the gauchos and their womenfolk in times past; acoustic instruments; and dance steps that correspond with the region the dancer represents. No piercings are to be seen on stage, let alone tattoos, rings, watches or plunging necklines. As the regulations state: "The dancers' boots ought to have reinforced sections on the front part of the soles, spur shanks at the back, must not have metal tips, and must be finished in traditional colours. The 'foal shoes' ought to be authentic in design, though they needn't be made from the same materials as originally (horse or puma hide). The use of daggers is not permitted, and neither is the presence of *boleadoras* [a lariat with stones instead of a noose], spears, spurs, or any other element not connected with the dance... The musical accompaniment must also be respectful of tradition in every regard, and must comprise no more than two instruments, one of which must be the guitar... The presentation must avoid all suggestion of sensationalism."

It is this uncompromising spirit that has probably done most to keep Laborde under wraps. In February 2007 Laura Falcoff, a journalist who had been attending the festival for years, wrote the following in the Argentinian daily *Clarín*: "Last January was the fortieth anniversary of the Laborde National Malambo Festival in Córdoba province, a festival that is to all intents secret, judging by the column inches dedicated to it in the mainstream press. For malambistas from across the country, though, Laborde is an out-and-out Mecca, the place on the map on which, once a year, centre all their hopes." Even in articles expressly focusing on the panoply of traditional dance festivals in Argentina, which are particularly numerous in austral summer, Laborde is almost never mentioned, and this in spite of the fact it falls right at the beginning of January.

The Malambo category is divided into two subcategories: the Quartets, in which four men dance in perfect synchronicity, and the Soloists. Within these come age categories too: Under Nines, Teens, Advanced Teens, and Veterans, but the jewel in the crown is the Senior Soloist category for male dancers who are twenty years and older. No more than five of these competitors try out each day. In their first appearance, usually at around one o'clock in the morning, they'll dance the "strong" malambo corresponding with the area they hail from. Next, at around three o'clock in the morning, comes the "return", with those who danced *norteño* before presenting a *sureño*, and vice versa. The jury meets to deliberate at midday on the Sunday, drawing up a list of finalists which is then passed on to the regional delegates, who in turn communicate the news to the competitors. Events reach their high point in the early hours of the Monday, when the three, four or five finalists dance the strong malambo pertaining to their own region. And at around 5.30 a.m., as the sky grows light over a still-packed exhibition ground, the winners of each of the categories are announced. The champion is the last to be announced. A man who is crowned and destroyed in the same instant.

———————————

ROUTE 11 IS A THIN STRIP of asphalt, intersected every now and then by rusty bridges over which trains no longer pass. To travel along it in austral summer – January or February – is to see the pampas in their picture-postcard state, bursting with all the different greens of the unripe wheat. The day is Thursday, 13th January 2011, and the entrance to Laborde could hardly be more prominent: next to a painted Argentinian flag – the sky-blue, the white – is the legend *"Laborde Capital Nacional del Malambo"*. The town's limits are also clear to see: it is seven blocks long and fourteen wide. There being nothing more to the place, people hardly know the names of the streets, getting around instead by indications such as "opposite López's house", or "next to the ice cream parlour". Similarly, the competition is simply held at "the grounds". This is where, at four in the afternoon, with the light dry like plaster, the only moving things in Laborde are to be found. Everywhere else has shut down: the houses, the newspaper stands, the clothes shops, the greengrocers, the supermarkets, the restaurants, the cybercafés, the corner stores, the rotisseries, the church, the town hall, the neighbour- hood centres, the police- and fire stations – as though a kind of paralysis had taken hold, a mummification even. My first thought on seeing these low houses with their cement benches outside, the unlocked bicycles leant against trees, cars with their windows left rolled down, is that I've seen hundreds of towns just like it, and what could possibly be going on here that is of any note?

UNLIKE THE FESTIVALS in Cosquín and La Sierra, malambo is the only featured dance in Laborde, and, also unlike other venues, where two or three minutes is the allotted time, here the dance lasts for five minutes.

Five minutes is hardly an eternity. A negligible amount of time when compared with a twelve-hour flight, a mere breath in a three-day marathon. But not so if the right comparisons are applied. The fastest one hundred-metre runners in the world aim for sub-ten second times; Usain Bolt's record stands, at the time of writing, at 9.58 seconds. A malambo dancer in full flow moves his feet just as quickly as a one hundred-metre runner, only he has to keep it up for five minutes. A malambo dancer's preparation therefore involves not only the sort of artistic instruction a ballet dancer would undergo, but also the physical and psychological preparations of an athlete. They don't smoke or drink, and they never go out late. Long-distance running and time in the gym are standard, and the aspiring malambista also has to work to perfect his concentration levels and develop the correct attitude: a keen sense of conviction and self-confidence is vital. Though some train alone, most employ a coach, usually a past champion – whose hourly fees and travel costs they are obliged to cover.

Add to this gym membership fees, consultations with nutritionists and sports scientists, healthy food, and of course the attire – which can cost anywhere between US$600 and $800 for each outfit. A pair of the *norteño* boots alone costs $140 – and, given the punishment they receive, needs replacing every four or six months. There is also the annual trip to Laborde itself, which often means a stay of two weeks. Most of the contestants are from working-class families, with housewives, municipal workers, metal workers and police officers for parents. The more fortunate give dance classes, but there are plenty of part-time electricians, bricklayers and mechanics among them. A few will win the first time they enter, but for almost all it is a question of coming back, year after year.

As for the prize, the winner can expect neither cash nor a holiday, neither a house nor a car, but simply a rather plain trophy crafted by a local artisan. Laborde's true prize cannot be seen with the eyes: uppermost in everybody's thoughts are the prestige and recognition, the endorsement and respect, and the huge honour that come with being one of the best among the select few even able to dance this murderous dance. In the small, courtier-like circle of traditional dance devotees, a Laborde champion becomes a demigod.

And yet… In order to preserve Laborde's prestige,

and affirm its elite nature, a tacit pact has been in place between Laborde champions since the festival's inception: though they may go and compete elsewhere, they may never enter the Laborde festival again, or dance the solo malambo at other festivals. Should anyone break this pact – there have been two or three exceptions – they'll suffer the utter contempt and scorn of their peers. So the malambo a man dances to win will also be one of his last: the summit scaled by a Laborde champion is also the end.

In January 2011 I went to Laborde with the simple plan of telling the story of this festival, and of trying to understand why people take part in such a thing: fighting your way to the top, only to come straight back down again.

_____

ORANGE AWNINGS line the earth-packed streets around the venue. When night falls the stalls will open and start selling handicrafts, shirts, CDs, but at this hour they shine and glimmer in the bright sunlight. Wire fences ring the grounds, and just inside and to the right is a room called the Champions' Gallery, where photos of past winners are displayed. Next along are some food stalls that, later on in the day, will be selling *empanadas,* pizza, the stew known as *locro,* and rotis-serie chicken. To the left stand the toilets and the press room – a wide, square building with chairs, computers and a wall covered by a long mirror. And then, on the far side, the stage.

By the time I arrive I've heard a few stories: of this stage inspiring such awe in certain contestants that they change their minds minutes before going on, forfeiting the chance to take part; that a slight forward incline adds to the stage's forbidding air; that the ghosts of great malambistas past are so numerous that, for some, it can be quite overwhelming.

What I see is a blue curtain and, above and to the sides, sponsorship boards bearing the names of local companies. Microphones are positioned at the front, intended to amplify the sounds of every footfall with devilish precision. Before the stage stand the plastic chairs for the audience, hundreds of them, white, empty. At 4.30 p.m. it's difficult to imagine it in any state other than this: an empty stage and an island of plastic in the sun, heat waves shimmying upwards.

I'm looking up at the bough of a eucalyptus tree, with branches too sparse to block out the intense sun, when I hear it. A spaced-out gallop, or repeated gunfire.

Turning around I find a man up on the stage. With a beard, one of the wide-brimmed hats, a red waistcoat beneath a blue jacket, a pair of bright white *cribo* trousers, and one of the *chiripá* skirts in beige, he's practising the steps of the malambo that he'll dance tonight. To begin with he moves his feet, if not slowly, then still at a human pace – a pace one might match. Then he turns it up a notch. Then another, and another, faster and faster, until finally the man stamps his foot one last time, and stands with his gaze fixed for a moment on a point somewhere behind me, before dropping his head. At this point he also starts to breathe, or rather to gasp like a fish, heaving in and out for air.

"Good," says his accompanist, a man with a guitar.

———————————

WHAT COULD MOTIVATE A TOWN of immigrants who have resolved to make this place the end of their travels, a conservative group evidently given to neatness, to promote a dance associated with a class of person, the gaucho, best known for nomadism, rebelliousness and the rejection of authority? I don't know. But the Laborde National Malambo Festival is the same as any world cup in any discipline: it is a seal of unsurpassable quality, and whoever wins is the best in the world. Any dictionary will list several definitions for the word "champion" – a person who comes first in a competition, a person who stands in defence of a cause or doctrine, a hero made famous in battle, a knight who took part in single combat in olden times – and it seems that each of these could be applied to the winner in Laborde.

AT SIX O'CLOCK in the evening the scene is quite changed. The bars have opened and, throughout the town, groups gather on street corners and perform improvised dances to the plucking of guitars. They all seem very young and, though they wear baggy jeans, and though there are miniskirts and band T-shirts in evidence, certain details are out of keeping with their ages, and indeed the age: the boys have long hair and bulky beards, as the gauchos of the past would have done – or as they would in their received image, and the girls, as would their *paisana* forebears, wear their long hair in braids.

By eight o'clock, the roads leading to the grounds have been shut off. Inside, a large crowd mills about in the fair: stands selling the sweet *alfajor* biscuits, home-made cakes and pastries, shower curtains, dog coats, leather belts, *maté*, silver jewellery, knives, shirts. The food stalls serve portion after portion of the *locro* and barbecued meat and slices of pizza. The white plastic chairs are all occupied already and, up on the stage, the first competitive dances are under way. At this moment it's the Under Nines Quartets, diminutive gauchos whose youth wins them no concessions when it comes to the applause or indifference of the crowd.

Ariel Ávalos sits in a room that serves as a sort of festival library. A Laborde champion in 2000, hailing from the province of Santa Fe, Ariel is a rarity in that he wears his hair short and has only the lightest smattering of beard.

"There's no actual rule prohibiting you from taking part in other festivals, but there is an unspoken agreement between those of us who have been past champions. No other festival's as important as Laborde, getting ready takes years. And the way to show you value it is to not compete elsewhere. It's a way of saying that nowhere else is as prestigious or important."

Ávalos's father worked in a ceramics factory, and his mother was a housewife. He began dancing at the age of eight in dance workshops in his school and, in 1996, embarked on preparations for Laborde. The year he won, he trained under the 1987 champion, Víctor Cortez, a sports physician and nutritionist. He had to give up university, where he was studying anthropology, so he could earn a wage as a mechanic and thus pay Cortez.

"University was always going to be there, but the possibility of winning Laborde, no. You come here for the glory, not the money. But when you dance, your whole body boils, every single inch of you. You're on fire. The city I'm from, San Lorenzo, is on a river. I'd go down there and dance, watching the river go by. The force of the river is the same as what I felt dancing. The first obstacle a malambista has to overcome is fear: am I going to finish the malambo well? Will I have enough in me? Can I take it? When I was doing my training this psychology student gave me an exercise to do: I had to stand in front of the mirror and say 'I am the champion.' And until you believe it, you have to carry on saying it. I started in the bathroom mirror – 'I'm the champion, I'm the champion' – and to begin with I made myself laugh. But the day came when I believed it. Another one was imagining the moment the announcer said my name, giving myself those goose bumps. Even now, seeing the boys up there dancing, I want it to be me. I find it hard to believe there are people who don't dance malambo. But the training is incredibly tough. You need to be as fit as a professional footballer, except you'd never catch any footballer running as hard as they can for five minutes without a break. A footballer runs a hundred metres and has a break. A malambista keeps that up for five minutes. It kills you. A minute and a half in, your quads start to burn, and you start needing more air. And if you aren't prepared for that change in your breathing, you have to stop."

"Why?"

"Because you'll suffocate."

Ariel Ávalos was a finalist in 1998 and came runner-up (the only other award in the Senior Soloist category) in 1999. The runner-up always arrives as one of the favourites the following year, and so, after twelve months of rigorous training, he set out for Laborde on 3rd January 2000. A few days earlier, his grandfather had begun to complain of back pains. The grandfather had raised Ávalos from the age of thirteen, owing to the smallness of his parental home – Ávalos was child number three. But, following his arrival in Laborde, each time he rang home to let his family know how he was getting on, they'd say the grandfather was out, that the doctor had advised lots of walking and he was out stretching his legs. On the opening night in Laborde Ávalos kicked off proceedings, as is traditional for the previous year's runner-up, and went on to reach the final. In the early hours of the Monday, he left the stage exultant, knowing he'd danced well. He was backstage, recovering, when his trainer told him what everyone else already knew: his grandfather was in critical condition, he was in hospital; they'd decided not to tell Ávalos in case it made him want to pull out. Ávalos wasn't angry: he understood that this was how it had to be. At five o'clock in the morning on 17th January came the announcement of the champion's name, and it was him. He went out and said his thanks, danced a couple of figures – as is traditional – and after saying a few words, left the stage and sped off in his car for San Lorenzo. But his grandfather died at eight o'clock that morning, while he was still on the road.

"My aunt, who was the last to speak to him before he went into a coma, told me: 'Before he passed away he asked after you, he asked how you'd got on.' Those were his dying words."

Outside it's started to rain but, through the half-open door, I can see the audience in their seats, and none of them is budging.

"A malambista has to be ready to give up more than you can possibly imagine."

———————————

BY ELEVEN O'CLOCK in the evening the rain has stopped. A provincial delegation is on stage and, moving between some chairs, a group of ordinary-looking men and women not in costume – in jeans and skirts, shorts, with berets and ponchos – are dancing and waving handkerchiefs. It isn't a group of useless amateurs, but rather the whirling flower of the *zamba* dance. Laborde takes great pride in the crowds it attracts, because they hold the knowledge and power to discern what they're seeing – to judge the hits and misses. For them, Laborde isn't a museum for ossified traditions but a sublime display of something they grew up around, and which they continue to help flourish.

———————————

BACKSTAGE, in a space with an untiled floor and hollow brick walls, stand the changing rooms. Four of these are monastic cells with sheet metal doors and a single cement table inside, nothing more. The fifth changing room is off in one corner, with a gap between the top of its walls and the ceiling, and in this case with no table and no light of its own. There are two toilets whose doors don't shut properly, and a long mirror lining one of the walls. The eye-watering aroma of muscle balm fills the space, a hive of comings and goings, people in various states of undress, putting make-up on, stretching muscles, applying sprays, braiding hair, trimming beards – all of them on edge, waiting. There are numerous clothes racks bearing dresses and gaucho costumes, there are men in under-clothes, and women demurely manoeuvring bras off or on. In advance of their stage calls dozens of people do their warm-ups as the adrenaline pounds, blasting electricity into their inflamed hearts.

"No I *can't* get it off, idiot. This ring! I'm gonna kill myself."

A girl with impeccable braids, wearing a charm-ing flower print dress with voluminous shoulder ruf-fles, is wrestling with an enormous, fuchsia pink ring. One swollen finger, and five minutes before she's due to dance. The ring would mean automatic disqual-ification.

"You've used soap?"

"Yes!"

"And your spit, and washing-up liquid?"

"Yes, yes, it's not coming off!"

"Ninny."

On a bench to one side, a young guy is using a plastic bag to help slide his foot into his pointed-heel boots.

"It's to make them slip in. You can't do it otherwise. We always use boots two sizes too small – it gives us better control to have them so tight."

On the floor in front of the wall mirror is a long wooden plank. Four dancers, the members of a *norteño* quartet, are standing side by side on the plank, jutting out their chins and rehearsing haughty, defiant glares. Four chests rise up like the breasts of four cockerels preparing to fight. What follows resembles nothing so much as a section of the North Korean army on parade: astonishingly synchronized strides, and eight heels catching, stamping and scraping the floor – as though they were one single heel. An interested circle forms around them, other dancers quietly contemplating the moves. When the quartet comes to a stop, there's a sudden, frozen moment of rapture, before the circle disbands – as though it had never been there, as though what just happened was a sacred, or secret, ceremony, or both.

An hour later, at midnight, the doors to the five changing rooms are all shut and, on the other side of these battered metal sheets, noises can be heard, now drums, now guitars, now the most unalloyed of silences. There, standing to attention, are the men that all of Laborde is waiting for. Five of the dancers in the Senior Soloist category.

———————————

THE SENIOR SOLOISTS are announced in the same way each evening. Between 12.30 and 1 a.m., the Laborde Anthem plays – *Baila el malambo / Argentina siente que su pueblo está vivo / Laborde está llamando a fiesta, al malambo nacional* (Dancing the malambo / Argentina feels the pulse of its people / Laborde calls for celebration, for our country's malambo) – and the announcer's voice rings out:

"Ladies and gentlemen! The moment you, Laborde, and all of Argentina has been waiting for!"

The announcer always makes a point of including the rest of the country, for all that the rest of the country seems unlikely to ever find out.

"Ladies and gentlemen, Laborde, the entire nation… it's time for the Senior Soloist category!"

As the music fades, fireworks burst into the sky. And then, the moment the announcer says the name of the first dancer, the silence is total, as if there's been a sudden snowfall.

———————————

THE MEMBERS OF THE JURY, at a long table immediately in front of the stage, sit stock-still.

First there is the sound of a guitar being strummed, conjuring all the sadness of the final days of summer. The dancer is dressed in a black corduroy jacket and red waistcoat. The white *cribo* coats his calves like a creamy rain and, in place of a *chiripá*, he wears a dark, tight-fitting girdle. Fair hair, full beard. He makes his way to the centre of the stage and stops, before, with movements that seem to burst from deep in his bones, using his toe to stroke the boards, then his heel, then the flanks of his foot – a trickle of precise taps, a series of perfect sounds. As in the moments before a wolf is about to strike, the tension builds as the dancer increases the pace – soon his feet themselves become two animals, tearing into the stage, grinding it, splitting it into pieces, hacking, shredding, devouring. The final time he brings his foot down, it's like two trains colliding. The dancer stands still. Bathed in sweat, he stands rigidly staring out, with all the severity of a lofty, tragic chord. He bows and moves off stage. Then a woman's voice, deadpan and impenetrable:

"Time: four minutes and forty seconds."

This was the first Senior Soloist Malambo I saw in Laborde, and it shook me. I dashed backstage and caught a glimpse of the man – Ariel Pérez, the Buenos

Aires candidate – diving into his changing room with the urgency of someone who has to hide that they are in love, or that they hate a person, or that they have been having murderous thoughts.

———————

"AY, LOOK AT YOUR TOE!"

Irma puts her head in her hands and stares at the toe in question, which, poking out the end of the "foal shoe" bindings, is enormous, and has a gash in the tip.

"I know, Ma, it's nothing."

"What do you mean nothing? It's almost falling off! I'm getting bandage and disinfectant."

"Oh, come on."

Irma ignores her son and goes looking for the first aid box. The boy, Pablo Albornoz, is sitting in a chair, and looks at the toe as though this isn't the first time he's seen it like this. Twenty-four years old, he's representing the province of Neuquén, having been under the tutelage of Ariel Ávalos, and is far more concerned with recovering his breath – he'll be dancing for the second time in an hour – than with the toe.

"Doesn't it hurt?" I say.

"Yes, but when you're up there you're so juiced you don't even notice. It's four and a half minutes and you just go all out."

He works as a caretaker at a kindergarten, and has competed at Laborde numerous times already – so many times that he wonders whether he's really any good.

"I must not be! I've been dancing since I was twelve, but there are some who've been dancing for four years and they show up in Laborde and win on their first try. But I'd also die if I couldn't come."

Irma returns with a vial of sterilizer and a cloth. Crouching down, she considers the toe, under which a pool of blood is starting to collect.

"Ay," she says. "There's a whole piece missing."

"All right, Ma, all right. We'll look at it later. Now I have to dance."

Irma douses and bandages the toe, Pablo puts on his boots, using the plastic bag, and goes over to one side of the room to stretch off. A toe in bandages, a plastic bag, boots two sizes too small: not precisely what you could call glamorous.

"I always come with him," says Irma. "It is tough, the bus trip is really long, arriving here at eight o'clock in the morning on the Monday, and he had a rehearsal slot at eleven, so it was off the bus and straight here. Another day his rehearsal slot was 4 a.m. to 6 a.m. He puts everything into it. He has to pay his tutor, including his plane tickets, then there's our rooms, classes, and the outfits of course. But if they do win, it changes their work prospects totally, because then they can be someone else's tutor, take on students, sit on juries. Pablo's young, he's only twenty-four, but you have to win before you're thirty, or that's it."

In Laborde the concept of "ex-champion" doesn't exist – whoever wins, reigns forever – but the title means, along with eternal prestige, more work and better pay. A dance teacher, or someone with a degree in folk customs, no matter how good they are, will never be paid the $200 a champion would get for a day of classes, or for being on a jury. So, while out on the stage others dance, and people in the audience watch, applaud, eat and take photos, in here, behind the stage, wreathed in the smell of arnica and muscle balms, they await the moment when, perhaps, their lives are going to change forever.

"People of Laborde, and Argentina!" says the announcer. "These are the sons of the nation, they uphold our traditions!… Time for a short break now, and we'll be right back."

HERNÁN VILLAGRA lives in a town called Los Altos, in Catamarca, is twenty-four years of age, studies criminology, and hopes one day to become a policeman – his father is a policeman – and he is constantly in pain. Today, Friday, sitting at a table in the bar on the corner of the square, he's in pain; when he gets up to go to the bathroom, he's in pain. The pain accompanies him wherever he goes because he has osteoarthritis in his toes and the solution is to operate, but first there's a rite he has to complete: to go up on stage and dance the last solo malambo he'll ever dance in Laborde. Villagra is the 2010 champion, which means he's spent the whole of the past year travelling, giving interviews and signing autographs. In the early hours of Monday he'll bid farewell to his kingdom and hand over the trophy to the new champion, who from that moment on will receive all the attention he's been receiving.

"I've been dancing since I was six. I first entered Laborde in 2007 – I was terrified. You can't be just anyone to dance on this stage. The day we got here my tutor said to me, 'Change into your outfit, we're going to rehearse on stage.' There were a few other guys up there going through their steps, and that was when the nerves started. I fell ill that same day, totally fell apart, started vomiting. But I danced anyway and it turned out pretty well. I got to the final, though I didn't win. In 2008 I came runner-up. And in 2009 I came runner-up again – being runner-up more than once starts to get embarrassing. I'd rather have lost than come runner-up again. It was awful. Being so close but not making it over the line. Plus your thoughts start turning to the year ahead, all the work you're going to have to put in if you want to come back, and over time, physically you just start to wear down. It's five minutes and you pound those boards. Your legs suffer, the tendons, all the cartilage, every inch of you is in pain. Dancing the *norteño* means guaranteed blisters, and the *sureño* makes your toes burn when you're dragging them across the stage, plus the boards always give you splinters."

"And is it worth the pain?"

"The thing is, what you feel when you're up there is unlike anything. It's like electricity. I came back in 2010 and got to the final. And I ended up dancing the best malambo of my life. When I came off stage, I'd gone blind. I knew it was my best ever malambo. It was like I was in shock. And I won. When I went home as champion, people lined the streets, we did like a ten-mile-long procession."

"And now?"

"Now I just do anything so I don't have to think about my last malambo. I have to enjoy it, because it's my last. A lot of things must go through your head in that moment."

"What kind of things, do you think?"

"And so many emotions."

"Such as?"

"And everything that's happened this year."

"For example?"

"And the things I've been through."

I'm about to carry on asking, but I desist. I start to see there's no point.

———————

"SO MUCH GOES THROUGH your head." "You feel so many different things." "You never forget it." "You have to go up there thinking of yourself as champion." "To represent my province is already success for me." "People say the most amazing things to you."

The way the malambistas talk is somewhat similar to professional footballers, the phrases they trot out when they speak to journalists: "We've got a great group." "Team spirit is amazing." "They were the better team." When it comes to specific questions – what do they think about while they dance, what memories do they have of the night they won – they all come out with the same set phrases: they make reference to the huge amount that goes through their heads, or to how wonderful it all was, but rarely will they go into specifics. If someone pushes them to describe at least one of the wonderful things that happened to them, they'll tell the story of how, for example, the champion from 1996 came and gave them a hug and said, "Now you have to show you're worthy of that trophy", or about the little child, in a school in Patagonia, who trembled with emotion on being given an autograph. Maybe these things seem insignificant. For them – children from large families, raised in remote villages, living in the most strained economic circum-stances, and with no famous forebears – such things mean everything.

————————

"LOOK, THIS ONE'S shut too. These Laborders."

Carlos de Santis, the delegate from the Catamarca province, is driving around in search of a place to buy food. It's 12.36, and in Laborde everything shuts at 12.30 and doesn't open again until four or five o'clock. Even in the face of two thousand festival-goers, Laborde will not forego its siesta. Not that this is especially surprising to de Santis – a dance teacher and tutor of the only two

malambistas from Catamarca ever to win in Laborde –
Diego Argañaraz in 2006 and Hernán Villagra, whom
I've just been speaking to – hailing as he does from the
small village of Graneros in Tucumán province, population 1,000.

"I lived in a house with mud walls and a roof made
out of canes. We kept food cold in a well we made on the
roof, covering it over with a wet rag. I collected firewood
in the mountains to sell. Or I'd catch frogs and sell them.
I wanted to study, so that meant leaving the house at
five o'clock in the morning and walking three hours to
school. I'd get there at eight, classes lasted till midday,
then I'd get home at four. And at five I'd head outside to
work, until the sun went down. I worked in a bar in the
evenings, waiting tables, sweeping up, and they'd give
me a Milanese scallop and the tips. Someone came to
give a malambo demonstration in the village one day,
and I went along. I wanted to learn everything: malambo,
English, piano, anything just so I could get out of the
village. Not because I didn't love the village, but I didn't
want to end up ploughing the fields, spending the rest
of my days stuck out there on the mountainside. This is
why I think the malambo is so important to us. We're all
from poor families, we've all had hard lives. And that's
how the malambo is too. That's what the students need to
learn, that they have to express this essence. To defend

the tradition. But it's a great sacrifice, three hundred and sixty-five days preparing to dance that five minutes. A whole year's work, and if you make a mistake, it's gone just like that. And the boys are all from very modest backgrounds, it isn't easy for them."

At one o'clock, by which time it's clear that nowhere is open, Carlos de Santis pulls up in front of the Mariano Moreno school, where he and his delegation are staying.

"Come on, we'll show you around."

In the itchy heat of the playground, clothes have been hung out to dry and a few men sit playing cards. Inside, the school resembles a refugee camp. Fans, five of them, circulate the warm air around, the floor is covered with mattresses, and these in turn are piled with blankets, towels, hats, clothes, guitars, drums, and people. Someone has stuck posters up on the walls: "Please clean up after yourselves and keep the place tidy, for everyone's comfort." There are thermoses of tea strewn around, cups of *maté*, sachets of sugar, baby bottles, nappies, bottles of cheap fruit juice, jars of *dulce de leche*, tea bags, bread, biscuits. Ponchos have been hung in front of the windows to black out the day, and a number of women are ironing the evening's outfits. The heat is so dense it seems to darken the air. De Santis gestures towards a classroom in one corner:

"That's where I sleep," he says.

In that corner lies a mattress, and nothing more.

THE AVERAGE AGE is twenty-four. None of them drinks, smokes, or stays out late. Many of them listen to punk, heavy metal or rock, and they all know how to tell the difference between dances like a *pericón* and a *cueca*, a *vals* and a *vidala*. They're devoted readers of gaucho staples such as *Martín Fierro, Don Segundo Sombra* and *Juan Moreira*, which epitomize the tradition and the gaucho world. The saga formed by these books, and certain films of the era – such as *The Gaucho War* – are as inspiring to them as *Harry Potter* or *Star Trek*. They place weight on words such as respect, tradition, nation, the flag. Each of them aspires – both on stage and off it – to the supposed gaucho attributes: austerity, courage, pride, sincerity, forthrightness. They wish for themselves a certain ruggedness and strength, to face all that life will throw at them – which is, and always has been, a great deal.

HÉCTOR ARICÓ IS A DANCER, a choreographer, a researcher, and the author of numerous articles and books on traditional Argentinian dance. He has been a member of the Laborde jury for the last fifteen years, and his reputation is ironclad. Today, Friday, the same as every day, he's been at the jury table from eight o'clock in the evening to six in the morning. At ten he gave a talk on costumes. Just now he's smoking a cigarette beneath a parasol out in the grounds, dressed in black, and he modulates his speech with precision, gesticulating fulsomely – I'm reminded of a star of silent cinema.

"Laborde makes nowhere nearly as much money as other festivals, because that's the way the organizing committee and the delegates prefer it. But it's the bastion of malambo, and the ultimate accolade for any dancer."

"What does the jury look for in a dancer?"

"First and foremost, symmetry. It's a strictly symmetrical dance, when the structure of the human body is obviously anything but. The first training they undergo, and the hardest, is designed to bring about symmetry, for everything to be exactly the same on their left and right sides; they have to be just as skilful on both sides, just as intense – the sonority, and the way they occupy the space on either side, have to be the same. The second problem is stamina. They know three or four minutes won't cut it in Laborde, they have to last closer to five minutes. So we look at how much they're able to withstand. Next, the structure, which has to be pleasing to the eye while staying within the regulations: there are limits, for instance, to how high their foot lifts can go; this isn't a *show*," (Aricó uses the English), "it's a competition. And the musical accompaniment. It's quite common for the musicians to do too much, when all you really want is for them to back the dancers, not try and steal the show. Finally, dress: does the trim of a poncho correspond with the area the dancer is representing, do the *bombachas* have the right number of pleats? When one of these boys wins, a whole new market opens up for him, but at the same time, early retirement. They're champions at twenty-one, twenty-two, but in a dance they can never perform again. There aren't any rules expressly prohibiting it, but the thing that goes through their heads is, 'What if I enter another festival and lose? Better to hold on to the glory.'"

"ALL THE FEET COMING DOWN at exactly the same time, that's what I need from you guys."

In the early afternoon, as the sun beats down, a quartet is rehearsing on stage. They're barefoot, and wear garish shirts and Bermuda shorts.

"That's the one thing I need," the tutor says. "Together, together, together. All the feet, all at the same time."

And the four of them – together, together, together, all at the same time – bring their heels down on the boards as though intent on extracting a confession. Meanwhile, Pablo Sánchez, the Tucumán delegate, sitting in the shade of the eucalyptus trees, is addressing a group of boys and girls who listen with worried looks on their faces.

"We have to be strong. There are other festivals that are good, but Laborde is a different class. It's the heavyweight. This is the first time it's happened in fifty-five years of the dance, and you'll see soon enough: we'll get the money together for the bus. Don't worry yourselves about that – just give your all when you're up there dancing."

At a nod, the group of youngsters disperses. Sánchez, the patriarch of a family of Tucumán malambistas, tutor to six champions and two runners-up in his time, tells me that the bus they were meant to travel on, and for which they'd paid in advance, never showed up. They waited and waited, but finally had to book another bus – and pay all over again, of course.

"We're up to our ears in debt, but everything will be just fine."

"Didn't you think of calling off the trip?"

"Not for a second. Not coming to Laborde would be out of the question."

Sánchez's oldest son, Damián, was on track to become a great Laborde champion when, at the age of twenty, he died of a brain haemorrhage. Then, in 1995, the next son, Marcelo, entered and won.

"The power of the dance lies in the spirit, the heart. The external aspects – that's all just technical. The *repique* has to be perfect, you have to know how to do the lifts, how to land the instep, and go up and up in energy from start to finish – energy and attitude. But the malambo is a far more powerful expression than other dances. Which means, as well as the techniques, you have to be able to handle the wood, to feel it, to become a part of the stage. The day you lose that, you lose it all. You have to feel each and every blow. Like the heartbeat. The message has to come through, loud and clear, to the crowd."

"What's the message?"

"The message is: 'Here I am. I'm of this land.'"

———————————

"I NAMED HIM FAUSTO, after *Fausto*. I believe we creoles need to maintain the creole ways, however we can. Brian, Jonathan, I'm not going in for any of that. Anyway with my surname being Cortez, they wouldn't go."

As well as being Victor Cortez's son's name, *Fausto* is the name of a book written in the 1900s by Argentinian writer Estanislao del Campo, and an archetypal piece of gaucho literature. Cortez, representing Córdoba province, was champion in 1987, and was subsequently declared *persona non grata* by the organizing committee after he brought a lawsuit against them having lost his job as a teacher in the dance school the festival supports.

"Champions have certain privileges. They don't pay the entry fee, they eat for free while they're here. I have to pay to come in, I have to buy my food, but the worst thing is not being allowed backstage with the boys I've been teaching. It's like protecting a child the whole year round, then suddenly, at the very last second, dropping them into the abyss. Because that's the crucial moment – when you're putting your boots on, the gaucho outfit – that's when you feel the malambo swelling inside you."

Nowadays Cortez works as a welder for a bus-making company. He talks about how the other workers will occasionally come across an article about him, and how they can't believe it.

"'Look at this old guy we work with,' they say. 'Look who he is.'"

He's sitting on a bench in the main square. The surrounding bars are beginning to get busy, and on a central patch of grass groups of boys and girls are playing guitars and dancing. Cortez's charge this year is Rodrigo Heredia from Córdoba, and he's entering the Senior Soloist category for this first time.

"He's a fine creature. Wholesome, clean. You can make someone into an artist, but not a good person. When I came to Laborde I thought I was the best. If someone put me up in front of God I'd have said, 'I'm better than you.' And I mean, in a way that's what you want them to think, you need to make them think like that – you can't have them lose humility, but at the same time when they're up there they need to be able to say, 'I'm number one.'"

"And what if they lose?"

"It's hard. But life does go on."

———————

TIREDNESS KICKS IN at the two-minute mark. If someone has been trained to a standard level, they wouldn't be too hard pressed to dance a malambo for that amount of time. But after two minutes the only thing that sustains the body is training, along with the endorphins produced by the suffocating sensations, the contraction of the muscles, the aching joints, the expectant gaze of six thousand people – and a jury scrutinizing you until the final breath. Maybe this is why, when they leave the stage, the dancers all appear to have been through something unnameable, a cruel trance of some kind.

———————

IF DURING THE DAY the temperature can rise above 40°C, it also drops at night without fail. Today, Friday 14th, at half-past midnight, it must be around 13°C, but backstage, notwithstanding, it's carnival time. There are half-dressed bodies, sweat, music, and the sound of *corridas* being sung, the ubiquitous ballad songs. The La Rioja representative, Darío Flores, descends the stage in the usual manner: his vision blurry, his body crucified, he stares around, keeping his arms outstretched to encourage air back into his starved lungs. Someone hugs him, and he, seemingly coming out of a trance, simply says: "Thank you, thank you." Watching this, I think to myself that I'm becoming accustomed to the same agitated tension when they're in the changing rooms, the same passionate uproar when they go out on stage, the same agony and, each time, the very same ecstasy when it's time for them to come down. Then I hear a guitar being strummed out on the stage. The notes contain something – something akin to an animal inching along low to the ground, about to pounce – that grabs my attention. So I hurry back out, crouching as I go, and take a seat behind the jury.

It's my first sighting of Rodolfo González Alcántara.

And what I see strikes me dumb.

WHY, IF HE WAS LIKE many of the others? – beige jacket, grey waistcoat, one of the wide-brimmed hats, the *chiripá* in red, and a piece of black cord for a tie – and why, if I didn't yet know the difference between a very good dancer and a mediocre one? But there he was: Rodolfo González Alcántara, twenty-eight years old, representing La Pampa, towering over everyone – and there I was, sitting on the grass, speechless. When he finished his dance, the announcer declared in her deadpan voice:

"Time: four minutes and fifty-two seconds."

And that was the precise moment when this story became something else. A not at all simple story. The story of a common man.

———————

WHEN RODOLFO GONZÁLEZ ALCÁNTARA came on that Friday evening, he moved to centre stage like a strong wind or a puma, like a stag or a thief of souls, standing still for two or three beats, frowning as he fixed his gaze on something behind us, something no person could see. The first movement he made with his legs ruffled his *cribo* trousers like some delicate underwater creature. Then, for the ensuing four minutes and fifty-two seconds, the night became a thing that he pounded with his fist:

He became the countryside, the dry earth, the taut pampas horizon, he was the smell of horses, the sound of the sky in summer, and the hum of solitude – fury, illness, and war – he became the opposite of peace. He was the slashing knife, the cannibal, and a decree. At the end he stamped his foot with terrific force and stood, covered in stars, resplendent, staring through the peeling layers of night air. And, with a sidelong smile – like that of a prince, a vagabond, or a demon – he touched the brim of his hat. And was gone.

And that was it.

I don't know if people applauded. I can't remember.

WHAT DID I DO NEXT? This I do know because I wrote it down in my notes. I rushed backstage but, much as I tried to make him out in the general disorder – a giant of a man in one of the wide-brimmed hats and a red poncho, it shouldn't have been difficult – he was nowhere to be found. Until, in front of the open doors to one of the changing rooms, I saw a very short man, no more than five feet tall, without a jacket or waistcoat or hat. I knew it was him because he was gasping for air. No one was with him. I went over. I asked him where he came from.

"Santa Rosa, La Pampa…" he said – in a voice I would come to know well, along with that way of slightly downplaying his own words by cutting himself off at the end of phrases. "But I live in Buenos Aires. I teach dance."

He was trembling – his hands and legs trembled, his fingers when he ran them through his sparse beard – and I asked his name.

"Rodolfo. Rodolfo González Alcántara."

Then, according to my notes, the announcer said something that sounded like: "Molinos Marín, the flour that combats cholesterol." I didn't write anything else down that night. It was two o'clock in the morning.

———————

IT'S SATURDAY and I'm trailing after Fernando Castro and Sebastián Sayago. Castro is Rodolfo González Alcántara's trainer, as well as being his accompanist on guitar. He became champion in 2009 at the age of twenty-one – Sebastián Sayago, his older brother, is here this year dancing for Santiago del Estero, the most successful malambo province. They form a strange triangle: brother, trainer, opponent. Added to which, though the pair had known each other, as they say, "forever", Castro only found out at the age of nineteen that Sayago was his brother.

SEBASTIÁN SAYAGO is tall and thin. With his dark skin, dark eyes, and very dark hair and beard, he sits on the patio of the rented house he and seven others are sharing. He lives in Santiago, the capital of his province, with his mother and ten-year-old sister, Milena. He's been dancing since the age of four, is now twenty-six, and for the last five years has worked as a dancer on cruises – he presents malambo "spectaculars". Here in Laborde he's been sharing a bed with a dance colleague, because there's so little space.

"Some people ask me: 'Why do you want to go and dance in Laborde, when you could earn proper money out in the real world?' But they have no idea what it means to me. The stage in Laborde is unique. To be standing on those boards where all those souls, all those champions, have come before. Before I go up I always ask them to let me pass, to let me dance."

This is the third time he's entered the Senior Soloist category – he did so previously in 2006 and 2010, but has never made the final.

"This time I cancelled a load of contracts with the cruise company so I could be in Santiago, training. It's a sacrifice, because I help my mother and my sister, who's like my daughter, she's the apple of my eye, but it has to be done. I get up at 6 a.m., I go for a run, I practise. You have to work on attitude, being elegant, the aggressive look – presenting yourself like a gaucho. You spend hours in the mirror trying to find a face that's more temperamental. I try to make it so people can see I'm marking my territory, that I'm going to defend something. And when I go up I try to feel like I'm all lit up. Like every step is going to give people goose bumps. Generally you start at a slow pace, and then you introduce harder elements, getting faster as well to show your skill, precision, strength, and, lastly, your endurance levels. When you start to go very quickly, you give your heart to the malambo, because your muscles aren't any good any more, so then it's your soul you have to put into it – every single bit of you."

Sebastián's feet are thin and his skin dark – he's barefoot because of the blisters from dancing *norteño*, which always burst when he dances *sureño*.

"I left blood all over the boards, but when you're up there you don't feel the pain. You become a giant. You're this gigantic person out in the middle of an empty space."

His father left when his mother was pregnant with him, and Sebastián met the man when he was ten, by which time his father had another family – including, among the three children, Fernando Castro, the oldest.

"Fernando and I knew each other through the Santiago dance scene – the two of us danced tap. I knew he was my brother, everybody knew. Except him. Then one day someone said: 'You should greet your brother.' 'What brother?!' he said. 'Sebastián,' they said, and I went over and introduced myself."

"And then what did you say?"

"I put my hand on his shoulder and just said, 'That's right, Fer, have a seat, let's talk a bit.'"

"How did he take it?"

"Well, really well. We get on, Fer and me."

The year he won, Fernando Castro knocked Sebastián Sayago out in the pre-tournament qualifying stages, which meant that, in 2009, though he'd put in a great deal of preparation, Sayago couldn't take part in the festival.

"I was on a boat, in Australia, when I found out that Fer was champion. I was in my cabin, fourteen hours ahead, watching the whole thing on the laptop. I cried to myself."

"You were envious?"

"Not in the slightest. I felt joyful. Proud. Sad to not be there. If anyone from Santiago wins, that's the best, to me. Plus he's my brother, even better."

"And if you win what will you do with your trophy?"

"I'll give it to my grandfather."

FERNANDO CASTRO is in the press room, dressed in jeans and a red shirt beneath which what appears to be a rosary peeks out. His long hair is gathered in a bun, and he looks like he's just stepped out of the shower.

"It's important we give a good image. I was champion in 2009, so it's important I present myself well and avoid setting a bad example. People are always going to look to you if you've been a champion."

He's been dancing since he was ten and now lives in Buenos Aires, where he's studying for a degree in Argentine folk traditions, but finds the pace of the city too much. His house is in San Fernando, an area of the sprawling conurbation twenty-five miles from the city centre.

"I find it takes its toll, travelling into the city every day. I'm never on time. I miss Santiago. There I had my birdcages, siesta. In Buenos Aires everything's a hundred miles an hour. I don't like it. In Santiago I'd go fishing and bird trapping. I'm a very patient person, I spend hours fishing."

"What do you think about when you're fishing?"

"Nothing. I watch the way the water moves."

No one knew who Fernando Castro was when, aged twenty-one, he entered the Senior Soloist category.

Since he looks five or six years younger than his actual age, and is very short, people asked whether he was there for the Under Twenties special youth category. But his malambo hit people like a meteor. His preferred style is the *norteño*, and that year he gave his absolute all in a luminous, valiant, battery of a display that left everyone dazzled, and that wrested the cup from Hernán Villagra, the previous year's runner-up and the favourite.

"I had this little monkey face of mine to contend with. I was new, no one was backing me – no one – and I was this tiny guy. But I was totally prepared."

"Who trained you?"

"Nobody, me. I trained myself. I came up with my own method. I'd go out for runs thinking about malambo. I ran with attitude, I walked with attitude, I took a bath with attitude. I'd watch gaucho films, *Juan Moreira*, *Martín Fierro*, to help get into character; what was it like being a gaucho, what were the hardships they went through, how did they carry themselves? Because I had to get across the idea of a man, a gaucho, using only my smooth monkey face, no beard or anything. This beard you see has only just appeared and, what, it's all of three hairs? But when I danced, people got to their feet, they clapped, and I left the stage feeling really pleased. And then they made me champion. After that the interviews started, the TV, the radio, and I hardly said anything. I was very shy. No one ever showed me how to talk. I had to learn. And the next year, when I had to hand over the trophy, that was when all the emotion came flooding into me."

"What did you feel?"

"That it was the end of something. I can't dance now. Because they don't let me do it here. If it wasn't for that, I'd enter all the comps. But it's like a pact; it's something that upholds the title. If you go elsewhere and *don't win*, that would be like sullying Laborde. But I enjoy the way my students are like pieces of me, my eyes, my soul, my feet, when they're on stage."

"Does it bother you that so few people know about the festival?"

"No, no. There aren't many festivals like it, ones that uphold the traditions, ones that aren't all theatre, where it isn't all about the standing ovations – where they don't have amps for the guitars."

Fernando Castro was a skater, he practised judo, karate, and as well as folk music he listened to, and still listens to, punk – he likes the Argentine punk band Flema, and the rock bands El Otro Yo, Dos Minutos, and Andrés Calamaro. He says his friends always understood that, though he liked these other things, his abstemiousness was non-negotiable.

"I've tried alcohol in this last couple of years. But I've never been drunk. I'm here to represent my province, I can't go dragging Santiago del Estero through the mud."

His parents could never afford the journey to come and see him dance in Laborde, so the year he won his uncle, Enrique Castro, who had been undergoing cancer treatments, accompanied him.

"He gave me faith, he told me he would read the Bible and pray for me. He didn't know the first thing about malambo. Laborde was the first time he saw me dance, but it made a real impression on him. I go on stage and I feel like King Kong, I feel like I'm huge and everyone else is tiny. And I try and find this calm inside, I try and make it so that everything inside me goes very slowly, and outside I'm faster than everyone. Malambo for me is like a story. My malambo has twenty-three figures, each with its own mood. The first one is like the taster. That's when you see if you've got it, if you've got punch, quality, presence. And then it's like you're telling your story: this is everything I've been through."

"You've been through a lot?"

"I come from nothing. There's very little I haven't done for a bit of money. The only breadwinner in my house is my father, he drives the local bus in Santiago, and I've got two brothers – well, three. There's my other brother, Sebastián Sayago, my father's son by another woman. We knew each other from both being around, we both danced, but I never knew we were brothers, until one day one of the professors says to me, 'Say hi to your brother.' And I say: 'What brother?' 'Sebas,' he says. I went over to him, and it turned out he knew. It made me so proud knowing I had an older brother who was into the same stuff as me. And the thought of us both representing the province, and the country."

"You weren't angry with your father?"

"No, I really wasn't. I wondered why he hadn't told me. But I never brought it up with him. I never told him I'd found out, but after that he worked it out for himself. My younger brothers don't know Sebas is my brother. But I don't know if it's up to me to tell them. I feel like it isn't. I feel like my pa should do that, don't you?"

———

TWENTY-ONE, twenty-two, twenty-three years old. Each of them aspires – both on stage and off it – to the gaucho attributes: austerity, courage, pride, sincerity, forthrightness. They wish for themselves a certain ruggedness and strength, to face all that life will throw at them – which is, and always has been, a great deal.

––––––––––

IT'S SATURDAY NIGHT and the representative of
Mendoza province waits in changing room number 5 –
the one whose walls don't reach the ceiling. The door is
shut but the sound of the guitar emanates like a solid
substance: a belt of adrenaline and foreboding. When
his call comes, he walks through the backstage area
with a frown, avoiding all eye contact. And what I see is
the same thing I see every night, on all their faces: the
certainty that they are absolutely alone, and the relief
and trepidation that comes with knowing that this is it,
that their time has come at last.

––––––––––

ONE OF THE SENIOR SOLOISTS, as he prepares for
his *norteño*, reminds me of a bull preparing to gore a
man. That night, at four o'clock in the morning, the
bearing of one of the dancers when he comes on stage
is like that of a person declaring war on the universe:
he stands centre stage for a few seconds, legs astride,
the edges of his neckerchief caressing his chest with a
sort of mock-innocence. The first figures – his boots,

like everyone else's, have tacks stuck in the heels to amplify the sound – verge on the serene: the *bombacha* trousers ripple slowly, like the tentacles of a jellyfish, and the man, chin up, crosses his ankles and sweeps the ground with the soles of his feet, stops on his heels and whips around, holding his upper body erect all the while, following the movements as though this were quite natural, as though his body were a column of flesh and ivory. A minute and a half in, each time he spins around, his head is wreathed with a further ring of sweat. Three minutes in, and his malambo has become a wall of sound, the boots, drum and guitar blending together and accelerating to a dizzying pitch. Four minutes, and the dancer's feet are crashing furiously against the boards – guitar, drum and boots merging into a single, flurrying mass – and then, after four minutes and fifty seconds, the dancer drops his head, lifts one foot and, with almighty force, unloads it into the floor. His heart is beating monstrously quickly, and the expression on his face, both lucid and frenetic, is that of someone who has just received a revelation. After a few seconds standing sullen and still, amid roaring applause from the audience, the dancer, like someone emptying a few more shots into a dead body, moves back with several brief, furious taps, everything in him seeming to shout *this is what I am made of: there is nothing that I cannot do.*

SUNDAY, ELEVEN O'CLOCK in the morning. The finalists will be announced today, and the whole town is suf-
fused with that mixture of resignation and anxiety that
signals the end of a long wait.

Hugo "The Cheek" Moreyra, who hails from Santa Fe
and won in 2004, is at the festival grounds, sheltering
from a light shower under the awnings of the barbecue
stand. He's thirty-one and says of himself that now, like
all champions, he's become fat.

"The second you stop training you put on weight. You
can tell a past champion by the belly. No one's deter-
mined enough to say, 'I go to Laborde, I win the championship, and yet I carry on training for another three
years…'"

Moreyra isn't fat, but if you compare his current shape
with the bag of bones that won the championship seven
years earlier, there is a difference. More notable, in truth,
was the size of his belly in 2004, which was non-existent.

"I found winning a great relief. I'd entered the previous four years, and I came runner-up in 2003. I said: 'If I
don't win this year, that's it for me.' I was finding all the
practising really tough."

The son of a housewife and a metal worker, he's
danced since the age of four; his sister had a place in

the local ballet at the time, and when she fell ill one day, so as not to forfeit it, he stepped in. And the year he won at Laborde, he'd only actually had a five-month stretch of training, after a sprained ankle saw him in plaster and undergoing physiotherapy between the previous April and August.

"But nobody knew, and I wasn't going to tell them. As soon as they knew, they'd only start thinking I had no chance: 'Oh, poor boy, how can you possibly dance, surely you're going to struggle.' You give the others an advantage: it's different competing with someone who's just got over an injury to someone who's been train-ing all year long. But I ended up winning. Of course, winning Laborde chops your legs off. You're allowed to compete in the other categories, in the Combined Malambo, the Twosomes, but not as a Soloist. We come to win, knowing full well that also means losing. Plus it's only those of us who come to Laborde who know about Laborde – no one else has even heard of it."

"Would you like it to be better known?"

"No way. Us dancers, we know this is the pinnacle, and that's enough for us. You could have a degree, you could be a doctor, but if you're a Laborde champion, that beats everything."

Moreyra's phone rings. He answers, and after hang-ing up says to me:

"The names are out."

The finalists are: 2010 runner-up Gonzalo "El Pony" Molina, the entrant from Tucumán, the entrant from Buenos Aires, and Rodolfo González Alcántara who, like the previous year's runner-up, represents the province of La Pampa.

RODRIGO HEREDIA, twenty-three years old, with a beard and his long hair in a bun at his neck, and looking very tense, is part of one of a number of delegations staying in a building that was once an old people's home. He hasn't been at the social club – where, after the festival finishes every night, a dance takes place until eleven o'clock in the morning – hasn't drunk, and hasn't been to bed late. While in Laborde he maintains the same monkish rhythms as he does the rest of the year.

"You have to look after yourself. The tiniest thing, people will find out, and then you look bad."

Those taking part in the Senior Soloist category, along with past champions, keep to a code of conduct which complies with an old motto: appearances, as much as what you do, are of the utmost importance. Thus the

prestige of any competitor or champion will take a per-
manent hit if there are rumours of alcohol or drugs, or
even, if their dress or hygiene aren't impeccable.

It's mid-afternoon and Rodrigo, dressed in jeans and
a yellow shirt and standing in one of the old people's
home's gloomy corridors, tells me that the advantage
of staying here is the quiet, and that some rooms have
their own bathroom. His, in fact, doesn't, but there is a
mattress, a wardrobe, and, to one side, a travelling bag
into which his clothes have already been packed, including his gaucho outfit – which won't be seeing any further
use this year. Earlier, at midday, when his tutor learned
that Rodrigo hadn't made the final, he came and said to
him: "Son, I want to thank you for all that you've done
for me. The bad news is that we didn't make the final."
Rodrigo's answer: "I see. I only hope, sir, that I haven't
been a disappointment to you."

"First thing," says Rodrigo, "is to start saving up so
we can come back next year."

Twenty-one, twenty-two, twenty-three years old.
Each of them aspires – both on stage and off it – to the
gaucho attributes: austerity, courage, pride, sincerity,
forthrightness. They wish for themselves a certain ruggedness and strength, to face all that life will throw at
them – which is, and always has been, a great deal.

MARCOS PRATTO lives in Unquillo, where he sells art products, but he was born and grew up in Laborde, and is the only local ever to win the Senior Soloists.

"I trained under Víctor Cortez. I made the final in 2002, and won the following year. I was the only entrant from Laborde. There's never been another. But when I started dancing, when I was twelve, my friends all laughed, they thought malambo was for the oldies. Nowadays you see kids in the city going around with a guitar slung over their backs, dancing tap on the street corners, but it didn't used to be like that."

Thirty-two years old, middling in stature and with a surly look about him, he's currently sitting in the press room. As well as his job selling art products, he teaches malambo, but says he himself will never dance again in one of the other categories, citing his current "size" – he wants people to retain the impression they formed the year he won.

"But all this about abstaining from alcohol and not smoking, having to look after yourself and work the body, I don't think it ought to be seen as a sacrifice. That's what any person does if they want to achieve something, simple as that. And that's why I think it shows a lack of respect when the festival has the Senior

Soloists going on at four in the morning. The whole year, you're saying to the guy, 'train, don't go out late, eat well', and the day comes, the most important competition of his life, and you hand him the most hellish night shift ever. And the setup backstage is terrible: you're warming up and hundreds of people are swarming past, hundreds of people just coming in and using the bathrooms. Plus the organizers want champions to come back and be here every single year, but we get nothing for it. We have to pay our travel, rent a room. But on the other hand when I come, and I hear that music start up, I get goose bumps all over. I find it really emotional seeing the boys, all the dreams they have. For us it's the only seven, eight days of glory we'll ever touch. After that it's see you later, back to being a nobody."

"And could you, do you think, stay away one year?"

"Not a chance. I'd die."

COME SUNDAY NIGHT, an hour before he's due on stage to dance in the final, Rodolfo González Alcántara, alongside his trainer Fernando Castro, is getting dressed on the press room mezzanine: the changing rooms are all occupied. Rodolfo removes some clothes from a brown plastic bag and binds his feet, first with leather straps and then tape. He wets his hair. The knuckles of his toes are white with calluses, and his toenails are thick, almost wood-like. Half dressed – waistcoat, jacket and hat yet to come – he gets down from the mezzanine, approaches the wall mirror, and does a few steps. His gaze is distant, as though shielding himself from the flame that burns him. The steps complete, he says:

"Shall we?"

"Let's," says Fernando Castro.

A quartet has just come off stage and, backstage, there are euphoric embraces, the whiff of something having just gone very well. Someone points Rodolfo in the direction of a changing room, and he goes over and opens the door. Inside, asleep, is Hernán Villagra, who wakes and greets him.

"*Hola.*"

"*Hola.*"

And Villagra gets up and goes out. Fernando Castro puts the guitar to one side and surveys the pleats on Rodolfo's *chiripá*.

"It's long on this side and short on this side. Off."

Rodolfo removes the *chiripá*, and Castro, with the

utmost calm and attentiveness, as though he were dressing a child, or a bullfighter, adjusts the pleats, then the sash, and finally the string tie.

"All right?"

Rodolfo nods, but says nothing.

"Come on," says Castro, "enjoy it: it's the final." Then, as with all the accompanists, who have to be on stage before the dancer, he goes out, leaving Rodolfo alone with me.

Rodolfo begins limbering up, reminding me of a tiger in a cage. As he carries out his warm-up movements, he opens a bag and removes a book with blue flaps, placing it on the cement table in front of him and, without ceasing to move, begins reading. The book, I see, is a copy of the Bible and, leaning forward over it, he whispers the words to himself. He seems at once submissive, invincible and tremendously fragile. His neck is at an angle that seems to say, "I'm in your hands", and his fingers are interlaced in prayer. I watch from behind as this man, a man I know nothing about, readies himself to go out on stage, to lay everything on the line, and I feel, with an unforeseen and awkward certainty, that it is the most terrifyingly intimate situation I've ever been in with another human being. Something in him cries, "Don't look at me!" but the reason I'm there is to look. And so that is what I do.

A couple of minutes later Rodolfo shuts the book, kisses it, places it back inside the bag, and then turns on his phone, pressing play on a song – 'I Know You' by the Argentine rock band Almafuerte: *Come on, man, why throw your dreams away. / If you're not you, that will be the worst. / If you're not you, that will be the very worst.* It's 2.30 a.m. when Rodolfo finally goes out to dance.

HE COMES OFF STAGE bathed in sweat and makes his way directly to the changing room. Removing his jacket, he sits with his arms dangling between his legs. Fernando Castro comes through, accompanied by a short woman with long, glossy dark hair and almond-shaped eyes. Her name is Miriam Carrizo and, as well as being a dancer herself, she and Rodolfo have been together for the last nine years. They embrace and begin talking about things I still have no understanding of, like the rhythms and the figures. Then the wait begins – Rodolfo waits, Castro waits, Miriam Carrizo waits, and I wait.

At 6.30 a.m., as the sky grows light, Hernán Villagra dances his last malambo, tears flowing freely as he bids farewell to the crowd. Then come the epic tones of the announcement: Gonzalo "El Pony" Molina, representing the La Pampa province, is champion. And the runner-up, from the same province, is Rodolfo González Alcántara.

Two months are to pass before I see him again, this time in Buenos Aires.

———————————

THE FIRST THING I find surprising, I think, are the clothes. During the four days I spent in Laborde I only saw Rodolfo González Alcántara dressed as a gaucho. On this late March morning, in a Buenos Aires bar, I'm slightly shocked to see him in jeans – rolled up at the cuffs – and a black jacket, with a rucksack over his shoulder.

"Hi, how are you?"

Rodolfo is twenty-eight, has dark, not overly long frizzy hair, and a thin moustache. A sparse beard, concluding in a delicate line at his lower lip, gives him the look of a swordsman or a pirate. He has a square jaw, brown eyes – containing a constant sparkle of laughter – which, when he dances, spills out onto his face, producing a magnetism that seems reckless, suicidal even. It's eleven o'clock in the morning and he's just come away from visiting a nephew in the hospital. The bar is small, with old formica tables, and is situated in a fairly central neighbourhood, a few blocks from the IUNA – the National University of the Arts – where he took a degree in folklore, and where he now leads workshops in the Dance department. I ask him, though I know the answer, if it was the Bible he was reading that night in Laborde, and he tells me it was. Opening his black rucksack he takes out the same copy, with the blue flaps. He carries it with him everywhere, he says.

"I open it at random and read whatever I land on, and sometimes it's incredible, the thing I read is exactly to do with what's going on for me at that moment."

Currently he divides his time between giving classes at the IUNA, and at a number of other dance schools, and training under Fernando Castro.

"Were you happy to come runner-up?"

"Yes. Fernando and I looked back over my dances a lot, and there were some things that I let slip."

"What?"

"Towards the end my waistcoat began riding up – it got caught on my jacket. I realized when I went on stage, but I just said, oh well. I had confidence in my malambo. I got up there and I thought: 'This is mine.'

But I lost concentration, didn't end up giving it my all. Freddy Vacca, who won in 1996, told me: 'When you go up on stage, you have to have nothing left at the end. You empty yourself, and the crowd takes it all.'"

The crowd takes it all. Is that what I experienced?

———————

RODOLFO GONZÁLEZ ALCÁNTARA is biologically the child of a woman named María Luisa Alcántara and a man whose name he refuses to speak; for him, his stepfather, Rubén Carabajal, is his father. Rodolfo was named Luis Rodolfo Antonio González, but when he turned sixteen he went to his local registry office in Santa Rosa and asked them to get rid of the González. Since this wasn't allowed, he added his mother's name, Alcántara, making his full name Luis Rodolfo Antonio González Alcántara. His contact with his six brothers – two of them younger and four older – is sporadic. His mother and biological father married when they were fourteen and sixteen respectively: being the son of a radical evangelical couple who believed a man must take his first girlfriend as his wife, Rodolfo's father obeyed. The children came in quick succession – one, two, and

before they knew it, four. By the time María Luisa was
pregnant with the fifth, her husband had begun hitting
her – she still has the marks – but she was nonetheless
taken aback when he accused her of conceiving the
fifth with another man. Thus, pregnant, she left, taking
the four boys with her – plus the fifth inside her belly.
Rodolfo arrived on 13th February, 1983. Not long after,
his paternal grandmother took his older brothers – on an
excursion, she claimed – and never brought them back.
Rubén Carabajal was an eighteen-year-old bricklayer
at the time, knew María Luisa through her brothers,
and almost as soon as he heard that the woman he so
admired was on her own, he made his move. The baby
didn't bother him, or the four other children, but then he
was called up for military service. Rodolfo hadn't spoken
his first words yet when he came down with pneumonia
and, feverish and convulsive, had to be taken to hospital.
Rubén Carabajal found the perfect excuse to see María
Luisa and Rodolfo, alleviating the situation somewhat
by volunteering to donate blood and then stopping to
see them in hospital. At this point baby Rodolfo was so
bad he'd been taken to the monks to be anointed with
holy water (traditionally used to save dying babies from
entering Limbo). But Rodolfo made it through, Rubén
Carabajal finished his military service and went back to
working as a bricklayer, and they moved into a ten-foot

square, one-room house with a leaking tin roof. The toilet was outside, next to a well which they drew the water from. Two more children arrived: Diego, and a girl they named Chiri. At the age of twenty-seven María Luisa was diagnosed with arthritis and had to give up work. For long periods there was either nothing to eat, or only tortillas made of flour and water.

———————

AT THE AGE OF EIGHT, Rodolfo González was very short, very fat, and wanted to dance. Why? He doesn't know. No one else in his family had been a dancer, but he began taking classes with a man named Daniel Echaide while he was still in school – where he was a model student in spite of his parents' inability to buy books or comply with the smallest requirements: since there wasn't the money for the materials needed in the manual labour classes (in which they learned handicrafts and labouring skills), Rodolfo talks about taking planks meant for firewood and rubbing them down so he'd have something to write on, and then how during class he'd write his name, or draw the crests of football clubs, on the wood. His malambo tutelage under Daniel Echaide lasted two years, after which he joined a group called El Salitral, and after that, at the age of eleven, another called Mamüll Mapú, a traditional ballet troupe he stayed with for four years, touring festivals in Olavarría, Santa Fe and Córdoba, and winning them all. He was twelve when he first went to Laborde, entering the Junior category and experiencing something he'd never experienced before: he came second, which to him felt tantamount to not having competed at all. In 1996 he trained with the Mamüll group and, in the mornings, with Sergio Pérez of La Pampa, that year's champion, who offered to take Rodolfo on, free of charge. In 1997 Rodolfo re-entered in the same category and won. In 2000 he was champion in the Teens category, and in 2003 came runner-up in the Advanced Teens category.

In the meantime his parents had obtained a house through a government scheme called Own Effort: the state provided land and materials and the recipients had to build the house themselves. When Rodolfo completed secondary school – with excellent marks, as in primary school – he thought about trying to land a regular salary as a warden with the prison service. He had always worked, helping Rubén with building tasks, and had stolen corn from the fields to sell, but now he needed a stable income. He looked into the prison service's requirements and began to study for the entrance exam. One day a teacher said to him: "Are you sure? You're not like the others here, I can see you as a teacher, not in a prison. If there are things you're prevented from doing when you're young, you'll only pass them on to your children in the form of frustration, a sense of failure." The teacher's words affected Rodolfo, and before finding out the results of the exam – he was ultimately declared unfit due to a minor neurological irregularity – he knew it wasn't for him. In 2001 he travelled to a nearby town called Guatraché to give music classes in a secondary school. Early on, a supervisor from the IUNA was sent to monitor him, but Rodolfo was incensed by the idea that some other person could judge his work in this way, so he decided to move to Buenos Aires to study.

Following this first encounter in the bar, I walked Rodolfo to the IUNA. It was clear to me, as we said goodbye, that Rodolfo's story was that of a man in whom the most dangerous of emotions had been stirred up: hope.

A RUN-OF-THE-MILL MAN with run-of-the-mill parents struggling against run-of-the-mill hardship – or, at any rate, no worse than the hardships experienced by a great many poor families. Are we interested in reading stories like Rodolfo's? About people who believe that family is a good thing, that kindness exists, that God is real? Are we interested in the kind of poverty that isn't extreme misery, when it doesn't go hand in hand with violence, when it's free from the brutality we love to see and read about?

———————————

WHEN HE WAS FIVE he asked why his surname was González, when all his siblings were Carabajals. Rubén and María Luisa explained that his father lived far away with four of his brothers. Rodolfo and his biological father have always been distant. Not long ago he visited his older brothers in a place called General Pico, a city in La Pampa. His father was there and invited him for dinner. When they'd finished and were washing up, Rodolfo felt an impulse to hug the man. Rodolfo made to do so, but then told himself: "No". And since then Rodolfo hasn't felt that impulse again – he won't allow himself to. It's not a feeling he likes.

WE MEET AGAIN in the same bar. The day is cold and cloudy, but Rodolfo, who's visiting his nephew in the hospital again, is wearing the same black jacket as before, with just a T-shirt underneath.

"My mother left my old man for my sake, that's obvious. And that's why, to me, she's gold. She was my everything. But now I'm older I can see my father's side too. He was sixteen, he was a ladies' man, he played guitar. My mother loved him, she gave everything for him, but one day he turns around and he's got four kids, and another one on the way! He must have just thought: 'No way.' My mother's still got marks on her face, and that kind of thing is unforgivable, but nowadays I think, who am I to forgive anyone anyway?"

"Are you angry at him?"

"No."

Rodolfo isn't a bitter person. Hate, resentment, simply don't register with him. The nephew in the hospital is his older brother's son and he worries for him as though he were his own. His maternal grandfather died of gangrene after a thorn got stuck in his foot, but what Rodolfo holds on to is the image of Rubén Carabajal carrying him on his shoulders to see his dying grandfather, and his grandfather giving Rodolfo his handkerchief. Rodolfo grew up in a house that would regularly flood after rain, but what he remembers is the fun he and his friends had sheltering under the table and splashing around in puddles. There was no electricity, but Rodolfo laughs remembering how they used to play with the candles. He never had money to buy trainers but proudly recounts the story of Rubén Carabajal sewing up and lending the boy his own, which were newer, and then Rodolfo going and destroying them by playing football.

"I had a beautiful childhood. The thing was feeling hungry. In all the places I lived, really, I remember being hungry."

The year he chose to move to Buenos Aires, to begin his studies at the IUNA, was the hardest in Argentina's recent past. In December 2001 the socio-economic situation took a sudden, dire turn that was to see people dying in the streets, savers pounding on the doors of banks that wouldn't let them have their money, and unemployment at twenty-one per cent. Rodolfo arrived in February 2002, at nineteen years of age, in a city unfamiliar not only to him but also to his friends and family, where there was no work, and which was a powder keg.

"I was in Santa Rosa," he tells me, "packing my bags, about to go and get the train, and my father looked at me and said: 'Are you sure about this, son? How about we help you out here until you get yourself some work?'

That depressed me. But I said: 'No, no, I have to go. I want to study.' I came and lived in the halls they provide for Pampas students – I'd walk from there to the IUNA each day. The halls are in Constitución, so that's about sixty blocks, and coming back there at night could be rough, but I didn't have the money to take the bus. I couldn't get a job. Every now and then my mother would send me credits for the Trueque."

The Club del Trueque was a coinless exchange system which did well in those years. Participants could swap goods or pay with credits – a coin issued by the club itself that was redeemable nationwide.

"But in La Pampa one credit was worth a peso, and here it was four credits to the peso. That would buy me half a kilo of sugar. When they sent me money, I'd save it to buy fresh bread, sometimes a bit of mincemeat. The hard thing is having only rice with milk, or polenta with milk, or flour with milk, when the guy along from you is having a Milanese scallop."

The first time he went out in Buenos Aires at night a friend took him to Plaza Miserere. Miserere is the epicentre of the Barrio Once, a popular neighbourhood where a lot of homeless people gather at night. Rodolfo's first taste of the Buenos Aires nightlife ended with him being slammed up against a wall and frisked by the police.

"No one had ever asked to see my documents before, I'd never even seen the police close up, but the moment they saw us they stopped us and asked for our IDs. My eyes were red because of all the fumes, the dust and sun – I get an allergy; they just thought I was stoned out of my mind. They had us up against a wall and started patting us down. When they found my eye drops they took that as proof – you *must* be a stoner. But when I showed them my documents they let us go. I remember there were some transvestites in the street, and them asking the cops for a cigarette, and the cops *giving* them cigarettes… I couldn't make sense of anything. Dear God, I thought, what have I got myself into?"

In time, he secured a job in a factory where they made cases for spectacles, and on a building site where the workers had to hide whenever the inspectors showed up – no one had the regulation protective clothing. One day a friend told him he wanted to introduce him to a great dancer and took him to a traditional ballet called La Rebelión. Rodolfo was introduced to a bald man covered in tattoos, dressed in high-laced boots and ripped, baggy trousers – the company director. Rodolfo asked himself: "This is the great dancer?" Carlos Medina was the man's name, and indeed it was he whom Rodolfo's friend had wanted him to meet. Rodolfo and Medina went on to become good friends. Rodolfo began going along to La Rebelión and formed a dance partnership with a young woman who, like him, was quite short, and was five years his senior. Her name was Miriam Carrizo. For him the attraction was instant, but she refused his advances for eight months. He persisted, however, and eventually she agreed to go out with him. She left the young women's hostel where she'd been living, and Rodolfo left his student digs, and they got a place together in Pablo Podestá, out in the Bonaerense conurbation.

"I was sitting down at home the other day," Rodolfo tells me. "Looking around at the furniture in the living room, I remembered buying it all, buying the stereo. Each tiny thing took a huge effort. We'd buy one thing and that might mean we'd have nothing left over for groceries. I remember it being high summer and saying to her, 'Hey, we're going to go and buy ourselves a fan, just a small one.' We ended up getting this turbo-charged one, massive. And when we got home she said to me, 'Rodo, have you got any money for food?' And I said, 'No, have you?' 'No.' I remember we died laughing. Sometimes we didn't even have money for the train. I've got a pair of trainers with these smooth soles. So while Miriam was buying her ticket, I'd take a run up and slide under the turnstile in the metro. One time we had fifty centavos each, just enough for both of us to get the bus home. But to get to the bus stop we needed to take the train, and if we paid for the train we wouldn't have enough left for the bus. Since it was the last train that night, we both got on without paying. We're about to pull in to the station when the inspector appears: 'Tickets!' We gave him what we had and then walked the thirty blocks home, at one o'clock in the morning. But that isn't so hard to take. What's hard is when you don't have enough to eat. Arriving home and seeing there's nothing in the cupboard, seeing her crying from the hunger. That's hard."

After he graduated, Rodolfo began teaching at the IUNA. He secured a number of private students and a few hours teaching at a primary school elsewhere in the conurbation. All of which brought a certain amount of stability, though not a lot.

———————

HE LIKES TO READ, though only in the last few years has he had the money to buy books. At that point he went out and bought Shakespeare's *Complete Works*, the *Iliad* (which explained references to Achilles' heel to him), the *Odyssey* and *Oedipus Rex* (where he found out all he needed to know about the Oedipus complex, concluding that he himself had never suffered from it). He doesn't have Internet at his house and isn't used to email, but his text messages are very exact. One, from June 2011, reads: *Hello, Leila, would you be able to send me your email address? I need to ask you a question.* Another, from July: *Hello, Leila, we didn't see each other on Saturday and I've been worried about you. I hope everything is all right with you.* He's always prepared to learn from things that people say to him. One day he told me about being invited to give classes in a city a long way away, and when I asked if he was going by plane or bus, he said bus. I said that perhaps now, being a Laborde runner-up, he could agree better terms. And then, a few months later, we were on the phone and he told me he had made a decision about a certain job, because, "As you said, maybe I can agree better terms now." He has a good memory and he's appreciative. He still has the poem that the Guatraché director of culture wrote for him, and it still moves him whenever he reads it. It makes him sad that people in big cities work so much that they only see their children when they're sleeping. He prays before bed, he goes to mass, he says, with feeling, "Thank God" ("My parents are well, thank God"; "I've got plenty of work on, thank God"), but he's vehemently opposed to Church dogma and avoids religious ceremonies presided over by priests "who still believe God will punish you if you don't go to mass". At the end of secondary school he didn't have the money to go on the graduating trip, but he's thankful that his dancing has taken him to places such as Bariloche, places he'd never have made it to under his own steam. When he tells a story he does so like all good oral storytellers: he takes time, knows how to generate suspense, and he's an excellent mimic, for instance imitating perfectly a friend who fell in a ditch when they were out in La Pampa hunting *peludos* (a kind of armadillo). Rodolfo is stubborn and incorruptible. He once rang up a boot-making factory, the one he always bought his boots from, and told them he needed a pair for a certain date. They answered that they could only have them for him by 15th December. He needed them sooner; could they not do him the favour? They said no, so he went and bought a pair elsewhere. Two weeks later the original factory rang to say a malambista had failed to collect a pair of boots: if Rodolfo wanted, he could take those. His first thought was to try and sell the pair he'd just bought. But then he took a decision: if he'd asked a favour of them when he needed it, and they hadn't been able to help him out, he shouldn't now buy the boots. So he said, "No, thank you", and reconciled himself to his new boots (no easy thing, as they had square toes, whereas he had always danced in boots with rounded toes). When addressing someone younger than himself, or someone he holds dear, he uses the affectionate Argentinian "Pa", "Papi" or "Papito", and he uses the formal *usted* form for anyone ten years older than himself, unless he knows them extremely well. In 2009 he spent a few days in Santa Rosa. A neighbour asked if he wanted to take on some work in the fields, and he, not having any money at the time, accepted. The work consisted of gathering up wheat that had fallen over the sides of the harvester and shovelling it back down a funnel, so that none would be wasted. It was two ten-hour days under a blistering sun, working alongside Uncle Ramón, who was old but tough – who never once complained, which meant that Rodolfo, out of pride, didn't say a word either. It was the worst job of his life, but he recounts it as an entertaining episode. Ask him what he thinks of politics and he'll tell you that the politicians, whether on the left or the right, have no real interest in poor people: "At best, they sometimes give us what we need, but they never show us how to get the things we need for ourselves. That means they always have us by the balls." He's read most of Che Guevara's writings and, though he says he's no activist himself, he's moved by the story of "that asthmatic doctor who had the courage to do what he did".

IN 2011, Rodolfo's average day looks like this: up at six o'clock in the morning, breakfast, an hour and a half by bus to San Fernando, the neighbourhood where Fernando Castro, his coach, lives, and then a two-hour training session. From there, on Tuesdays and Thursdays, he goes to the secondary school in Laferrere to teach music to eleven- to thirteen-year-olds, and then, from Laferrere, onwards to González Catán to teach a traditional ballet class between six and nine o'clock in the evening. The two-and-a-half-hour homeward journey takes in three different forms of transport. On Wednesdays and Fridays he teaches until four o'clock in the afternoon at the IUNA, and then, until nine o'clock, in a ballet centre in Benavídez. On Sundays and Mondays he teaches traditional dance in Merlo and Dorrego. San Fernando, Laferrere, González Catán, Merlo, Dorrego, Benavídez: all of these places are a long way from where he lives, as well as being a long way from one another, scattered across a metropolitan area whose levels of hostility are legendary: the Bonaerense conurbation, with its population of approximately twenty-two million souls.

"From Fernando's house I take the number 21 bus to Liniers, then change to the 218 to Laferrere. When I'm done at the school, I take the 218 to González Catán, where the ballet is. It's the 218 again to come home – changing at Liniers and getting the 237. But if I'm not too broke, I take the Costera [a slightly more upmarket bus], get off at Márquez y Perón and take the 169 home from there. The other day, in Benavídez, I finished late, about ten at night, and it isn't safe to go out around there at that hour, so I ended up sleeping at the house of the student where I give the class. Sometimes the teaching assistants say to me, 'Why do you want to go and teach layabouts like that? If when they leave your class they just go and get high?' But I say, a layabout who comes to my classes is going to come out wanting to do music. So why shouldn't I?"

IT'S JUNE: midwinter in Argentina. It's ten o'clock in the morning and, in his house in Pablo Podestá, Rodolfo is preparing *maté*. He's put out a tray of toast, *dulce de leche* and butter on the dining-room table. The house, which belongs to Miriam's parents – a retired petro-chemical worker and his dressmaker wife, who live in Caleta Olivia, a small city in Patagonia – has a garden with fruit trees, two bedrooms, a bathroom, and it's recently been repainted.

"We did it ourselves," says Rodolfo. "Costs a fortune otherwise."

There's a picture of Jesus up in the kitchen, with the legend: *Jesus, I put my trust in you*. Up on a shelf in the dining room there's a photo of the couple, with the following words across the top: *For eternal life together*.

"There used to be a cement mixer behind us in the picture. But I took it to a photo shop, and the guy added that blue patch in the background. Now it looks nice."

"Is it peaceful around here?"

"Yes, sometimes things go on, but it's pretty peaceful, thank God."

Once, the year they moved here, they saw one of their neighbours shot – a man on a motorbike came flying round the corner and emptied three bullets into him on the kerb. The only thing Miriam and Rodolfo could think to do was turn off the lights and stay quietly inside the house while the man on the motorbike fled.

"The señora was shouting: 'My husband's been killed, my husband's been killed.' But Miriam and I were on our own here, we didn't have anyone. So we just stood by."

Rodolfo turns on the computer and clicks on some malambo videos he's lined up. He's going to show me how to distinguish the mistakes from the sublime moves.

"Malambo has slow, medium and fast sections; it starts slow and gets faster. As it gets faster, the moves become harder to execute, but it also gives you the chance to show more quality. You have to accompany the change from slow to medium pace with a change in your attitude, and then in the last part just shut your eyes, say 'God help me', and get your legs really moving. Look, see this guy's shoulders, the way they're becoming hunched? You have to avoid that. No need for the shoulders to hunch up like that. Now the crowd is starting to shout and clap, and you can see it on his face: he's starting to smile. The idea isn't for the crowd to lift you, but for *you* to lift them. And here, see the way he's breathing, gasping for air? You can't do that. When it comes to the last step of the malambo, it's like you plunge right down into the boards, then you can stand tall, chest up, and always breathing through your nose. If you breathe through your mouth you're done for, you're gasping and people can tell how tired you are – like with this guy. Breathing through your nose keeps you calm, and it means the audience doesn't know. No one has to know what you're going through."

No one has to know what you're going through.

———————

I'M WALKING WITH RODOLFO to the IUNA one day when he tells me about a dream he had, one he says he'll never forget. He was coming down the side of a sand dune onto a beach, and when he arrived at the sea, the tide started coming in. He tried to get back up the dune, but couldn't. There was somebody at the top, and he asked for their help, but the person said: "No, you can do it." He carried on trying to get off the beach until eventually his feet met solid rock, and he managed to get away. Then, from the top, he had a view over an enormous city. He jumped a wire fence and then he was in the city. He says he thinks the person at the top of the dune was God.

"And it's incredible," he says. "I went and opened my Bible, and the line I opened it at said 'God is our rock, and he supports us all.'"

Rodolfo, walking quickly, falls silent, as though he's feeling tense or his mind is busy with things he has to do. All of a sudden, he says:

"The hardest thing I find is, going up on stage and saying, 'This is mine'."

"Why?"

"Because it's immense. And that immensity frightens me. Anything endless, I panic. It's only in the last year

that I've become able to look at the sea. Stop in front of
the sea and look at the immensity and not be afraid."

———————

HE FINDS CERTAIN THINGS funny that to other
people could seem naive: he tells me how Gonzalo
Molina, "El Pony", with whom he's become friendly,
posted something on Facebook about "becoming a
father", and that the next day, dozens of congratulatory
posts later, Molina followed it up with another saying:
"My dog's having puppies." Rodolfo found this infinitely
funny. As for me, I must seem an imbecile, always asking
him the same question: why all this effort to try and win
a festival of such slender renown, why work so hard to
precipitate the end of your own career? I want to say,
but not explicitly, that being famous in the eyes of a few
thousand people doesn't seem worth giving everything
for. Time after time, and with great patience, he gives
me the same explanation:

"Being the champion in Laborde only means something to a very small circle of people, but for us, that *is*
glory. The year when you're champion, people want your
photo, they want to interview you, get your autograph.

And you want to make the most of that, because you aren't going to use your legs afterwards. When your legs are finished you have to use other tools. Laborde means you can be the man, but not the guy who wins so he can go and get all the ladies; instead someone who's demonstrated that working quietly, humbly, that way everything is possible. That's why I would like it if God would smile on me and help me to be mature, to be a man, so that I can go to Laborde in a good state and then give it my all. The first time I went to Laborde, the first time I stepped on that stage, I was hooked. And if that's what God wants, if God says to put this above everything else and make it your career, then fine. You give your all, and the winner takes all. But I don't want to be champion so I can be rich or see my face on a poster. I want to be champion because that's what I've wanted since I was twelve years of age, and finishing my career there would be just amazing."

OK, I always say, I see. But, deep down, I carry on asking myself how something so little known has the power to make a person say what this man says to me, time and again: that he marches, quite happily, towards his own demise.

"LET'S GO! *Racatá, racatá, racatá.*"

It's a June afternoon and Rodolfo is giving a class at the IUNA. The space is large, with wooden floors, mirrors and a piano. The students are like something out of a twenty-first century *Fame* – boys and girls in an array of headbands, tracksuit trousers, lycra shorts, leotards, and brightly coloured legwarmers. Rodolfo's in jeans – the cuffs rolled up – a black shirt and trainers.

"Take care over the facial expression," he says. "If you're doing *this*, it doesn't make sense for you to be laughing."

The *this* is accompanied with a stamp of the foot fit to crush a building and, although some of the students attempt to follow suit, the force which in Rodolfo appears natural, is still pure effort for them, a pretence.

"Come on, come on. You chose to be here. Let's go. *Racatá, racatá, racatá.*"

RODOLFO IS ALSO a discreet person. He never has a bad word to say about colleagues or competitors, and if he does ever mention someone by name, it's only to speak well of them: so-and-so always has a wise word, no one moves their feet like Professor So-and-so. Which is why I'm surprised when, in the bar one day, he tells me about a Laborde champion with whom he sat on a jury, and whose advice he asked about improving his 2011 performance.

"He said to me: 'Look, do your best, but it's going to be tough for you seeing as there's the runner-up, El Pony, who's from La Pampa. He's the favourite. You can be as prepared as you like, but when you're about to go on stage and you hear your name, and it's your turn, you get an absolute arse-full of questions...' And I said, 'Hmm, OK, thanks.' The next week I was giving blood, there was a kid at one of the schools where I teach, and he was in hospital over in Garrahan. You walk through the door, you see all those kids laid up in there, and *then* you get an arse-full of questions. For me, being Laborde champion is a huge dream. But if I don't win, I don't win. I don't want to be some guy who moves his legs but then afterwards can't string a sentence together. If I don't win in Laborde, I'll carry on going to the schools, to the IUNA. But I know where it is I get an arse-full of questions. And it isn't in Laborde."

Rodolfo hardly ever uses words like "arse" and, when he does use them, you can see the outrage in his face, and he looks down – hoping to hide, I suppose, something he doesn't want anyone to see.

"WITH RODO, what you see is what you get. He's so straight up."

Miriam Carrizo, Rodolfo's wife, studied teacher training in traditional dance. Though five years Rodolfo's senior, she appears far younger, with smooth olive skin and a gentle, childlike voice. Rodolfo both loves her and is somewhat in fear of her, because she'll tell him the things no one else dares to say: that he danced badly, that he wasn't focused, that his attitude wasn't right.

"Rodolfo wouldn't get angry if the sky fell on his head. He's very calm, very peaceful, very diplomatic. Yes, now and then things get to him, but he's always very respectful in the way he expresses it. And Laborde means the world to him. I've been through it all with him. We've had to make so many sacrifices, deny ourselves all kinds of things so there's enough to buy the next pair of boots. It means him leaving the house at seven and coming back at midnight, and me praying nothing happens to him. It means, on a Sunday, instead of the two of us going out for a nice walk, I'll go to the track with him so he can go jogging."

"Is it a burden for you?"

"Not at all. It's his dream, and I know if he wins it will be the happiest moment of his life. Of our life."

THROUGHOUT 2011 Rodolfo trained every day, rehearsing his steps as many as twelve times, going for hour-and-a-half runs, skipping, and doing sessions in the gym. He watched what he ate. He lost weight. And, come the first week of January, he went to Laborde looking to become champion.

On 27th December 2011, I received an email from Cecilia Lorenc Valcarce, the festival's press officer: *The Festival runs from the 10th to the 15th (early hours of the 16th). The opening dance on the first night will go to Rodolfo (in recognition of being runner-up).* From the Tuesday, therefore, through to midday on the Sunday, Rodolfo has to remain in Laborde, not knowing if he's through to the final or not. I, of course, will be there with him.

"RODOLFO, IT'S LEILA."

"Leila, hi, how are you?"

"I'm fine, you?"

"Fine, thank God. I'm on the bus. I go to Río Cuarto and from there I get the Laborde bus."

"And your family are going?"

"Yes, everyone. The old man, my mother, my brother Diego, Chiri, the boys, my sister-in-law's sister..."

"And are they there?"

"No, next week they come..."

"And where will they stay?"

"They've hired a coach – it fits forty-five people. They couldn't pay to camp, it was going to cost them the earth, so they ended up borrowing some money and hiring the coach. They'll sleep in it too."

At the other end of the line, Rodolfo's voice sounds as though he's travelling with the top down, and he sounds radiant, triumphant.

———

IN THE SUMMER OF 2012 there was a severe drought in Argentina but, in the south of the province of Córdoba, some green fields could be seen. Still, the air was thick with dust, and this gave everything an unreal, ghostly tinge. On 9th January, a Monday, the day before the festival was set to commence, with the temperature at 45°C, Laborde suffered a power cut; from one o'clock in the afternoon onwards, no one had any electricity. Still in Buenos Aires myself, I rang Rodolfo to check how he was doing. "Chilly!" he laughed. He was staying in a rented house with a number of friends who had gone along to spur him on.

"Feeling good, calm?"

"Yes, calm. Thank God."

Rodolfo was set to dance on Tuesday 10th. That day, in the afternoon, I was making the drive over. At five o'clock, just before coming through a town called Firmat, the heavens unleashed a torrent. First, the wind drove a blinding curtain of dust across the land, followed by teeming rain. I pulled over and took refuge under the eaves of a building. A message came in from Cecilia Lorenc Valcarce, the press officer: *Where have you got to? The organizers are meeting here to decide if we should postpone. High winds. Everything blown away.* An hour later, once I was underway again, another message came through from Cecilia: *All malambo suspended until tomorrow.*

I thought about Rodolfo. This unexpected cancellation... I asked myself if this – in a situation where the tiniest detail can wreak havoc on the competitor's spirits – might not be very damaging. I sent him a message, but didn't get an answer. At eight o'clock in the evening I arrived in Monte Maíz, a town twelve miles short of Laborde. That was where I was to be staying, given that Laborde was, as always, fully booked.

———————

IT'S WEDNESDAY MORNING and I'm suffering the after-effects of the thought I had while travelling: how unsettling must it be for Rodolfo to have a journalist following him wherever he goes? In the controlled atmosphere around every participant in the run-up to the contest, might I not act like a huge, toxic bacterium? A pressure. Does Rodolfo know his story will be worth just as much to me if he doesn't win? And then again, would it be worth as much? At ten o'clock in the morning I call him and ask if it's all right to come and start working.

"Of course, dear. Come on over."

———————

AT MIDDAY, in spite of, or perhaps due to, yesterday's storm, the sky over Laborde is a clear pale blue. The house where Rodolfo is staying stands on the corner of Calle Estrada and Calle Avellaneda. A student of his – Álvaro Melián – is sharing with him, as well as Carlos Medina and a number of friends from the La Rebelión ballet group – Luis, Jonathan, Noelia, Priscilla and

Diana – who have come along to provide encouragement. In a couple of days they'll be joined by Javier, Graciela, Chiara – Miriam's brother, sister-in-law and niece – and Tonchi, a childhood friend. Miriam, who's dancing in the festival's opening ceremony, isn't allowed to stay there because of some bureaucratic complication relating to her ballet's insurance policy. Rodolfo's parents, their siblings Diego and Chiri, their nephews, the sister-in-law's sister and her husband and children, are all going to be staying in the coach, which is parked on the edge of Laborde's campsite. The house is large, with a kitchen, two bedrooms, a living room, a bathroom and, at the back, a patio. People's things are everywhere: ornaments, silverware, clothes in the wardrobes. Rodolfo and Fernando Castro are removing the layer of soil that yesterday's winds dumped on the patio table.

"Take a seat, dear, we'll have some tea. We just got in ourselves."

Rodolfo has been out at Mass and is wearing a T-shirt that says *No more violence: a message from God*. This year Fernando Castro is going to provide his guitar accompaniment, and El Pony will play the drum, which means his backing has great champion pedigree. He's going to wear the same blue suit as last year for the *norteño*, but for the *sureño* he'll be dressed completely differently.

The hat was given to him by his sister; the waistcoat was embroidered by a group of IUNA students; the neck tie belonged to El Pony (who wore it for his winning dance); the jacket to the father of a friend; the boots and the *chiripá* (the latter dark, with a red and ochre trim) are borrowed; the *rastra* belt, which features Rodolfo's initials, R.G.A., was made and given to him by Carlos Medina (who as well as being a dancer is an artisan); and the *cribo* by a woman in Santa Rosa.

"But the white shirt is mine!" he says, laughing, as he sews a leather chinstrap onto his hat. "The last one fell apart from being sweated into so much. They wanted to charge me a fortune here to do it. Luckily," he says, brandishing a thick needle and a pair of tweezers, "I brought my own tools."

Carlos Medina, a talkative man who always seems to be in a good mood and who always, day and night, wears a baseball cap, is brewing the tea. He tells me how Rodolfo's initials came to be included on the *rastra* belt.

"There were something like forty-five letters – Luis Rodolfo Antonio, and so on and so forth, so I said to him: 'Nitwit, give me three letters maximum. Otherwise we're going to end up with a miniskirt, not a *rastra*!'"

Over at another table, beneath a tree, a group of very young children are painting a banner:

> *You'll show them who you are*
> *They'll see what you're made of*
> *And that what's inside your heart*
> *Got you where you are*
> *Go, Rodo!*

The verse paraphrases a reggaeton song by Don Omar, one Rodolfo always listens to. The lines go:

> *I'll show them who I am*
> *They'll see what I'm made of*
> *And that what's inside my heart*
> *Got me where I am.*
> *They'll see me conquer*
> *They'll see me become champion*
> *Since I didn't win the prize*
> *They crowned me the king instead.*

"Did you get caught in the storm on the drive here?" Rodolfo asks.

"Yes," I say. "I had to pull over."

"Here everything blew away. Lots of tents in the campsite were carried off in the wind, but my parents, thank God, were safe inside the coach."

I wonder to myself how comfortable ten people can be in a coach without proper beds, and a wobbly toilet, but what I say is:

"Great."

AT MIDDAY EACH DAY, lunch is served for the regional delegations in the dining area of the Laborde Athletic and Cultural Recreation Club. A dance is held, informally known as the Canteen Club, with some people dancing and singing while the rest eat and converse at the tops of their voices. But when I arrive, the vast room is empty. Used plates and glasses line the long tables, and the man clearing up has devised a fail-safe method: he rolls up the paper tablecloths, gathering the plates, cups and food inside, making a big roulade of plastic and leftovers. There are two or three people moving around inside the kitchens, and I head over to them.

"Anything left to eat?" I ask.

"Yes, have a seat."

I take a table with my bowl of noodle stew, and a tall man with dark hair comes over and asks to join me.

"Be my guest," I say.

The man's talkativeness, which at the same time has something austere to it that marks him out to me as a country person, is such that he strikes up a conversation with me as naturally as if, in a space with hundreds of tables and chairs available, he had asked if he could join me.

"I've represented my province for thirty-seven

years," he says. "Río Negro. Things have changed, for better and for worse. Once you'd see a boy from Corrientes dancing his malambo, and you'd know he was from Corrientes, the same if someone was from Buenos Aires. Now it's all much of a muchness, which comes of the champions travelling around the country and giving classes: all the different dancers end up dancing alike. And it's all become so athletic. Sometimes you see them dancing and they're like machines. The thing I value is the effort they put in, because they're from very humble backgrounds, the preparations take a lot out of them, and no one's guaranteeing anyone victory. Of course, the champion is set up for life. A hundred dollars per class – more, maybe – and after that it's see you later."

Before he gets up to go and take his siesta, I ask his name:

"Arnaldo Pérez. Goodbye."

Arnaldo Pérez. Río Negro champion, 1976. He was taught by a man who didn't know how to dance malambo, a historian who, after seeing him in a provincial competition, offered to give him classes, and thereafter would drive the 150 miles of dirt track roads to Pérez's house, and never charged him a single peso for his time. He's also one of this year's jury members. While we were speaking, before I knew who he was, I asked him what he thought of last year's runner-up, Rodolfo González Alcántara. Really, he said, not much.

———————

IT'S WEDNESDAY, midnight, and the scene backstage is as though this last year hadn't passed; the same carnivalesque uproar, the same women in voluminous skirts, the same small, sullen children standing around, the same faces: Sebastián Sayago – who's competing again this year and who will be dancing tonight – Hugo Moreyra, Ariel Ávalos, Hernán Villagra. Year on year the champions return, not only because it's expected, but because it's a pleasure to come back, and in many cases because they are training contestants. Someone has pasted the word MALAMBO, in flour, on the wall mirror. The announcer's voice rings out:

"And so, ladies and gentlemen – and the entire nation – there you have them, the Junior Malambo Quartets! The dreams of their teachers and parents, and all that hard work, are reflected in them! They are the seedbed, they are our future champions!..."

The Junior category is for ten- to thirteen-year-olds. The maximum time allowed for the dance is three minutes. Once the young dancers are finished, you tend to see them throwing themselves into their trainers' arms, crying disconsolately while the proud adults say, "That's it, cry, cry: that's how you're supposed to feel." At this moment, over to one side of the stage, there are several such children wrapped in their instructors' embraces, letting it all out.

It's 12.15 a.m. but Rodolfo has been in changing room number 4 since eleven o'clock. Removing his shirt, trousers and trainers, he takes a bottle of water and his costume out of a brown plastic bag. On go the shirt, the *cribo* trousers, the "foal shoe" bindings, the *chiripá*, the sash. Fernando Castro, already dressed in gaucho attire, contemplates Rodolfo in silence. And with the same calm attentiveness as the previous year, he sees to the folds in the *chiripá*, making sure they're even, and checks that the trims on either side line up. At 12.30 a.m. Rodolfo begins to stir, shifting his weight from one leg to the other, reminding me of nothing so much as a wild animal in a cage. Then he wets his hair, opens the bag, takes out the Bible, reads a little, whispering the words, puts the Bible away again, and takes out his mobile phone. On goes 'I Know You', the Almafuerte song. Fernando Castro, guitar in lap, says in a low voice:

"We're going to win, *compadre*. Bring out your ego, let all the joy come through."

Rodolfo nods, says nothing.

"Attitude, *hup*. Let it flow, do it, do it, *do it*."

Rodolfo sits down, though his limbs continue to move. Then, like last year, Fernando gets up and leaves, and it's just the two of us. And I'm not sure if I should stay, but I do.

———————

AT ONE O'CLOCK in the morning the Laborde anthem plays – 'Baila el Malambo' – followed by the voice of the announcer:

"Ladies and gentlemen, the moment you've all been waiting for! It's time for the category everyone wants to see! All of Laborde, and all of Argentina!"

When the fireworks go off, Rodolfo looks up and places the hat on his head. His face is that of a stony idol, that of someone who both is and is not Rodolfo.

"Ladies and gentlemen of the jury, champions, time for the Senior Soloist Malambo!"

Rodolfo pushes open the changing room door and walks towards the stage. He stands between the wing curtains, legs astride, back straight – as though readying himself before a kill.

"And now for a native of La Pampa! Put your hands together, and, as we say, light up your hearts, as we welcome last year's runner-up: it's... Rodolfo... González... Alcántara!"

The audience erupts. Cries can be heard – "Bravo!", "Come on, Rodo!", "Be strong!", "Go on, son!" – in amongst which I pick out Miriam's voice. Rodolfo, in the wings, stands still and makes the sign of the cross.

And out he goes.

———————

THE STRUMMING of Fernando Castro's guitar resembles a torrent of threats, a foretelling. It contains within it something of avalanches, something of stones, something of thunder: something of the world's end. Rodolfo comes on from the side, takes a few steps, before pausing to weigh up the magnitude of the task. Then, the remaining steps to centre stage, followed by three furtive, stalking paces towards the audience. He stands, feet apart, arms by his sides, fists clenched. Chords unreel from the guitar, emphatic and resounding, and Rodolfo stamps his feet upon the boards: *clack, clack*. And, from this moment on, the malambo that ensues takes place on a plane above the surface of the earth. Rodolfo's legs call to mind a pair of burning eagles and he, gone, no longer of this world, turns imposing, deadly, upright as a tree, clear as a jasmine breeze, rising with a kind of savagery above the delicate movements of the toes, subsiding, kicking out, roaring with all the archness of a feline, gliding along gracefully as a deer, becomes a landslide and at the same time the sea, the churning, crowning foam, before finally stamping his foot down one last time. There he stands: serene, pure, fearsome as a torrent of blood. In a cocky gesture, as if to say, "That was nothing", he straightens his jacket, before bowing, lightly tipping his hat, and turning and exiting the stage.

"Time," says that voice, deadpan as ever, "four minutes and forty-five seconds."

When I dash backstage what I find is a scorched-earth scene: Rodolfo and Fernando sharing a wordless embrace, like two men commiserating. Carlos Medina's eyes are glistening and Miriam Carrizo, with her arms around him, is crying freely. Something must have gone wrong, I think – something my untrained eye didn't catch. But then Rodolfo takes off his hat, huffs and puffs a bit, and Miriam goes over to hug him, saying: "Brilliant, Rodo. That was a good one."

Carlos Medina, who seems to be having trouble breathing, looks at me:

"I've never seen him dance like that."

Nearby, in the entrance to a changing room, Sebastián Sayago, who's on in a couple of minutes, is praying.

IT'S A LITTLE BEFORE TWO in the morning when Sebastián Sayago quits the stage – shouting:

"Shit, fuck, shit!"

His people form a circle around him, saying: "Let it out, that's it, let it out." But Sebastián looks furious – he grimaces like he's in pain. Someone gives him water, Rodolfo and Fernando go over and wish him the best. He vanishes not long after.

Rodolfo enters the changing room, removing jacket, waistcoat, the *rastra* belt. On his own, wearing just the white, billowing *cribo* trousers and shirt, he resembles a penitent or an altar boy. The entrants from Buenos Aires, San Luis and La Rioja are out on stage at this particular moment, while outside the changing room a group of girls from another delegation have formed a circle and are reciting, in unison, "Stretch, down, stretch, up" – as they stretch, bend down, stretch, and straighten back up again.

Rodolfo has a sip of water, takes off the shirt and the *cribo* trousers, and changes into the outfit for the return *norteño*. Once he's dressed, he goes out and runs through the entire malambo in the mirror – several people stop and watch in silence. Then he goes back into the changing room, and this time I stay outside taking notes. Next to me a little boy in full gaucho get-up is checking his mobile phone. A few minutes later the red-haired man who announces the dancing order dashes in:

"La Pampa, La Pampa!" he shouts. "Where's La Pampa?"

Since nobody says anything, I tell him:

"Changing room 4."

The man darts over and bangs on the door:

"La Pampa is up next in the Senior Soloists!"

This wasn't the plan: previously the running order had Rodolfo going on in half an hour or so, and I imagine this must be quite a shock. But a provincial delegation is still out on stage and I say to myself, *No problem, there's time...* Then I see Miriam come backstage, mobile phone to her ear and a tremendous look of anxiety on her face, and I know something's really wrong.

"What is it?"

"El Pony, he's supposed to be drumming for Rodo, but we can't find him!"

Miriam tries to get hold of El Pony, but he could be in any number of different places – having pizza, giving an interview, signing autographs, anywhere. With these crowds, and with the music playing, there's no way he'll hear his phone.

"What's happening?" Rodolfo asks.

"El Pony," Miriam says. "He's vanished."

How terrible, I think – though I don't know if I'm thinking this for Rodolfo, for me, or for the both of us.

———————————

LIKE SOMETHING out of a movie, three minutes before Rodolfo is due to go on, El Pony appears. Miriam is furious with the organizers, but Rodolfo puts on his hat and, with not a word to anyone, goes on. From behind I see him make his way over to the wings and cross himself. If, I think, his concentration was affected in the 2011 final because his waistcoat rode up inside his jacket, the havoc caused by this last-minute scare must be enormous. While I'm thinking these things, Rodolfo heads out and dances his *norteño*. When he's finished, that deadpan woman's voice:

"Time used: four minutes and thirty-two seconds."

Rodolfo exits the stage and comes past me, looking agitated. Miriam follows him into the changing room. She stands quietly looking at him, her brow furrowed, as though there's some secret she's trying to divine. Once Rodolfo has got his breath back, she says he didn't dance as she'd expected, that she thought the first two figures hadn't gone well, they didn't look good. Rodolfo agrees – he knows, he says, and he isn't happy either: the music didn't keep with him, he had the feeling when he finished that he hadn't given his all, and the scramble beforehand had made him nervous – he hadn't had time to focus. He takes off his jacket and boots and leaves the changing room. Outside, lots of people come over and embrace him, wish him luck. A young boy says he has something to give Rodolfo. He takes an object out of a plastic bag and hands it to him.

"Take it, it was my grandmother's."

It's a rosary. Rodolfo thanks the boy, kisses the rosary and places it around his neck.

THE NEXT DAY, the first piece of news I hear is that Sebastián Sayago injured himself during his dance and he's being given injections in case he makes the final. The second news I hear – a rumour – is that the jury was very taken with Rodolfo's performance. The third isn't so much news: I see Rodolfo and he tells me he's watched his *norteño* performance on video, and that it looked better than he thought. He's feeling calmer now.

"Shall we go and see my parents at the campsite?" he says.

"Let's," I say.

———————

THE COACH SAYS *ARIEL TOURS* along the side and is parked at the edge of the campsite, a green space full of tents on the far edge of Route 11. Rodolfo's parents, siblings and other relatives sleep inside the slightly dilapidated orange coach, but their days are spent in the campsite, whose facilities – barbecue, swimming pool, showers and toilets – they use in exchange for a few coins. Rubén Carabajal, a man of very few words, is sturdy and olive-skinned with a sparse beard. María Luisa Alcántara is a short woman – shorter than Rodolfo – very thin, with straight hair and fine, square features and small, sad eyes that seem to suggest she could be about to fall asleep at any moment. Her arthritis has left knots and bumps on her knees and hands.

"Rodo's a good boy, very responsible," she says, sitting on one of the campsite's cement benches, beside a table with a spread of *maté* and biscuits. "He was very sickly when he was little – pneumonia. He lived inside that hospital for a time. I stayed in with him, I had to wash his clothes there, I'd dry them in the little bathroom – I remember the nurse coming to me and saying, 'What's this, González, haven't you got any family?' Yes, I said, but they don't come. Just once they came, when Rodolfo had been given an hour to live. Rubén was the only one who came to see me; he got leave to come and donate blood and then stayed a bit. We went through so much together. So when Rodo told me he wanted to go to Buenos Aires, I felt like dying. He went at the worst time. But he said, I have to go, Ma, I'll never come to anything if I stay here. I had a nephew – he was killed seven years ago, shot – and he said to me: 'The only one who's got his balls in the right place is cousin Rodolfo, going to Buenos Aires when he was nineteen and didn't know a soul.'"

"Someone killed your nephew?"

"Yes, a block from my house. The area where I live is called 'Mataderos', after the slaughterhouses, and that's a very unfortunate name. It comes up on the GPS as 'danger zone'."

"When he left," says Rubén Carabajal, "we didn't have a peso to send him off with. What a time. I work for the council now, I do maintenance work, and we have a bit of money coming in. But in those days I was earning 150 pesos. Nothing."

"Didn't you think he might have been better off going and studying something other than dance, something with more secure prospects?"

"No," says María Luisa, "this was his dream. Having a national champion as your son is no small thing. He says: 'Ma, I'm doing something I love.' And I say: 'Well, son, it's important you're happy.' We always support him in everything. When he goes to Santa Rosa, and it's forty degrees outside, he goes for a ten-kilometre run. The house in Buenos Aires doesn't have proper flooring so he has to tap dance on concrete, with just his 'foal shoe' bindings on. Do you know what that's like? Poor boy, he works so hard. Sometimes I'll ring him at half-past midnight and he still won't be home yet, he'll be waiting on some train platform."

The conversation turns to the family legend: Rodolfo being so meek as a boy that he always got beaten up at school, until one day María Luisa said to him: "If you don't start hitting them back, all of them, next time you come home I'm going to start hitting you." Then the time they were so low on money that Rubén stole a pig and ended up in jail. And all the *peludo* hunts the men of the family would go on.

"Once they came back with twenty-five *peludos*," says María Luisa. "There was a time when the house was like a zoo. There were otters, lapwings, geese, ostriches. A little fox. One day the ostrich escaped – it ended up in our neighbour's pot."

"How did you know it was your neighbour's?"

"Because the mother told me – they found an ostrich, and they ate it."

She had a back operation in 2011, she was given a prosthesis, and now they're heavily in debt to the hospital – their medical insurance stopped short of hospitalization.

"Plus there's the coach to pay for. A neighbour lent us part of the money, the rest we borrowed from Chiri's husband. Right, Chiri?"

Chiri, who works as a house cleaner, and whose husband is a dustman, a fairly well-paid job in Argentina, is at this moment tending to a small baby.

"First thing is to pay your neighbours back," she says. "After that, we'll see."

María Luisa makes a face as if to say: *"We'll see."*

"God will help us through, I believe that."

"Are you staying for the barbecue?" Rubén asks me. "We've already put some on for you."

"Laborde has prompted you to rethink lots of things, made you reflect at a personal level, it's been good for you."

"Yes, yes, Laborde stimulates you in other ways. When you're up on stage, you leave a lot of emotion out there. For me it's been a great lesson, definitely a good thing, a before and after."

"Well, best of luck to you, Rodolfo. We hope to see you on stage after four o'clock in the morning on Sunday!"

"Thank you – and a hello to all my loved ones."

"We've been talking with Rodolfo González Alcántara, one of the most thoughtful and serious runners-up we've ever come across. He was talking about good changes, the way he's made the most of situations, and all the lessons he's learned."

I'm driving in the car when this interview with Rodolfo comes on the radio. Sometimes – quite often, in fact – this is what he does: generalizes like this. You feel like asking him where is it, where have you left the monster that devours you when you go on stage: where on earth do you keep it?

ON THE THURSDAY NIGHT, a large moon hangs in the sky.

The entrant from Tucumán comes off stage blind, charges through the backstage area and into the wrong changing room.

And that's all.

––––––––––––

ON THE FRIDAY MORNING a group of Senior Soloists are having their photo taken in the grounds when Héctor Aricó comes by.

"Ug-*ly!*" he calls out.

A large group of youths are taking photos on their mobile phones. I realize Rodolfo is the shortest out of everyone.

––––––––––––

AT SIX O'CLOCK in the evening on the Friday, Rodolfo's student Álvaro Melián has climbed onto one of the windowsills of the shared house, and is quietly watching the goings-on in the room. Fernando Castro is sitting on a sofa strewn with clothes, guitar in lap. Rodolfo stands in the middle of the empty space dressed in the *cribo* trousers, the *chiripá* sash and a blue shirt. One of his molars has been giving him trouble all day, and he has a swollen ankle. At the Laborde hospital they recommended an injection to bring the swelling down, plus some painkillers, but he didn't want either in case they affected his dancing. His mother offered him an analgesic and an anti-inflammatory. When Rodolfo came out to the campsite looking for them, he found Rubén sleeping down the middle of the aisle in the coach and his mother also asleep in one of the seats, her neck twisted over to one side, all in an asphyxiating heat. I later find out that the vignette made his stomach churn.

"I don't get it," he says now, bemoaning a figure he's struggling with. "I start counting it off from *here*, and it's from *here*."

Fernando Castro watches but says nothing, strumming the guitar. Rodolfo runs through the figure again and again. From time to time he'll pull up, and then Fernando speaks – as though trying to plunge him into a hypnotic trance.

"Think about what it's taken to come this far. Try to imagine you're in the final. Think about all the effort.

Think about the emotion, the adrenaline; imagine the moment they say your name and you go out on stage. You start by doing the necessary, getting it right. You end doing it from the heart, give it all your experience. Imagine everything around you is going very slowly, and you're going super fast. Come on now, from the top…"

Rodolfo leaves the room and comes back in, sparks in his eyes. His bare sole as it strikes the ground is like the crack of a whip.

"Feel like you're the champion, damn it!" cries Fernando.

Rodolfo runs through the whole malambo, but isn't satisfied. At the end, he says:

"It's my first rehearsal since I danced, and I'm finding aches I didn't even know I had. Tomorrow I want to do a good rehearsal, because this one was a piece of crap."

———

ON THE SATURDAY MORNING Tonchi, his childhood friend, arrives. And although the finalists are announced on Sunday, and that makes Saturday a day of waiting and nerves, Rodolfo does his rehearsal and everything turns out superbly well. After that: a lunch of noodles, a few phone calls from people offering words of encouragement, followed by some down time, and bed.

_____

I GO LOOKING FOR RODOLFO on Sunday morning but can't find him. At 11.20 a.m. he answers his phone and whispers that he's at Mass.

In the church there are several girls dressed up as gaucho womenfolk, and some of the men are dressed as gauchos. Rodolfo is in a white shirt and tracksuit trousers, and he's sitting in a pew with Miriam and Tonchi, who's a young man, short and with dark hair. Rodolfo, head lowered, joins the queue for communion. A little later, after the closing words, the priest asks for a big round of applause for everyone taking part in the festival.

"*Viva la patria!*"

The congregation respond with a "*Viva!*" so loud it shakes the stained glass.

Afterwards, we go back to the house.

TONCHI, REAL NAME GASTÓN, has danced malambo since he was a boy.

"I danced jazz, tango. I've got a Francisco of Xuxo costume. I played Francisco of Xuxo in a school play."

Tonchi and Rodolfo are sitting out on the patio drinking *maté*, and, for a little while, the pair of them seem to forget the reason they're there: waiting for the call from the La Pampa representative to tell them if Rodolfo's made the final or not.

"When I saw this guy in the Mamüll, I didn't know what to make of him," says Rodolfo. "We didn't even say hello. Then we started dancing together, him, me and two of my cousins. Four dwarfs we were. I was a fatty, a real tub. But we pissed a lot of people off."

"When we went for the competition in Bahía Blanca they almost ran us out of town," says Tonchi. "We grabbed limes and hid, and then threw them at the people."

"You were very young?"

"No, like thirteen."

"And do you remember the way we used to dance?" says Rodolfo. "I moved like I was in plaster cast, and I remember Tonchi kicking down like he was trying to start a motorbike."

And like a pre-rehearsed skit, they get up and dance an atrocious, clowning malambo, flailing around with their arms, enormous forced grins on their faces. They sit back down, still howling with laughter.

"Idiot," says Tonchi, drying his eyes. "You'll kill me."

Tonchi was born with a congenital kidney problem. He's already had two transplants and is on a waiting list for a third. He has to do dialysis three times a week, between midday and four o'clock, and after that he goes to the gym, runs, and takes malambo classes.

"Dialysis is from twelve till four, that's the end of it. If you become all woe-is-me, *please not more dialysis*, you're done for. My renal function has been becoming much harder. I'm lucky that I pass urine every morning. Not much, but it comes through. Some people don't pass anything from one dialysis to the next. Dancing, and sweating, helps me a lot. But I don't take that much notice of the illness. Last year I tore a stomach muscle when I was out for a run in Bariloche. It hurt like hell, and I had no idea what was wrong. And they were about to operate, they were going to take my appendix out, and Rodo rings me and I tell him, 'Rodo, here I am, they're going to operate on my appendix.' And Rodo says, 'No, Pa, you don't *have* an appendix, they took it out already when you were little.' So I told the doctor,

'Doc, I don't have one any more.' I don't have a clue when it comes to illnesses."

Tonchi has a right arm like a tree root, with bumps and swellings all across it – from the dialysis. Before Laborde he was given a preventative diuretic treatment to compensate for the sessions he'd be skipping by being here.

"But I didn't make it last year, and this year I couldn't let Rodo down. Right, Rodo?"

"Yes, Tonchi, my friend."

Rodolfo is continually glancing at his phone. At midday we hear footsteps coming along the side of the house. We all waited impatiently, until the face of a bearded young man appeared round the corner.

"Hi all."

"Hey, Freddy," says Rodolfo. "Pull up a pew."

Freddy Vacca was champion in 1996, representing Tucumán. He's come to say hello and offer support, he says.

"Any word?"

"No, not yet."

They talk about Tuesday's storm, the old people's home, the canteen, the club, the heat, the power cut, the drought; the conversation involves a strategic skirting around of everything to do with the competition, and this seems to me, like so much else that goes on here, a sort of tacit code. After a little while, Vacca gets up from his seat.

"All the best then, Rodo," he says. "And remember, I'm up there with you, dancing inside your dance, eh?"

Rodolfo hugs him, thanks him for coming.

"Lovely man, Freddy," he says after Vacca has gone.

Twelve thirty p.m. comes around and still no call. Rodolfo suggests a trip to the campsite – his parents are lighting the barbecue.

"Maybe we'll get the call when we're over there."

"Rodo," says Tonchi, "before we go, would you peel a peach for me?"

"Yes, Pa, I'll do it."

Tonchi loves peaches but is allergic to the skin. Inside the house, as Rodolfo is peeling, I hear someone ask him:

"And, Rodo, how are you?"

"Nervous."

————————————

IN THE CAR ON THE WAY to the campsite, Rodolfo says:

"I thought it was going to be like last year, and we'd know by midday."

When we get to the main road the phone rings and

Rodolfo answers, his voice firm but with an urgency to it, an edginess.

"Hello?"

It's Carlos, Miriam's father.

"No, Carlitos, still nothing."

The campsite resembles the stage set for a happy moment in a play or a film. The pool is full of children, smoke rises from the barbecues. Rodolfo hoists nephews and nieces aloft, greets siblings and parents. At one o'clock I send a message to Cecilia Lorenc Valcarce – *Anything?* – and get one back – *Still nothing*.

"I'M SO NERVOUS."

Rodolfo is sitting on a bench and, in a confessional tone, trying to keep his voice down so his parents won't hear, again he says:

"So nervous."

Then we hear a vibration. Rodolfo reaches into his bag, takes the phone out, looks at it and says:

"Message from José Luis Furriol."

The La Pampa representative.

It's 1.40 p.m.

AND WHAT HAPPENS NOW?

How does it all end?

Does it all end?

IN THE TIME between Rodolfo receiving the message and reading it, my Dictaphone registers a long silence, as though the universe had stopped to contemplate how it is that three words might contain a man's whole destiny.

Rodolfo presses the button on his phone, reads the message and, in a clear, modest voice, says:

"I'm in the final."

His mother cries out, Miriam cries out, his brothers cry out, the whole campsite – everywhere people are shouting "Go, Rodo!" and "Up La Pampa!" José Luis Furriol's message will later end up lost after Rodolfo mislays the phone, but what it says is: *Rodolfo you are in.* As people shout and hug one another I call Cecilia Lorenc Valcarce to find out who else has made it through. The names I get back are: Maximiliano

Castillo (Río Negro) and Sebastián Sayago (Santiago del Estero) – the last of course being the brother of Fernando Castro.

I leave shortly after. We agree that I'll come by the house at eleven o'clock tonight to take Rodolfo to the grounds. On my way back to the car I feel touched by the privilege: I'm going to drive him there. Me.

Am I perhaps beginning to understand something?

WHEN I ARRIVE at the house that night, Miriam and Fernando Castro are also there. The atmosphere is sombre: in this town where nothing ever happens, Carlos Medina and a number of others from the shared house have had their jackets stolen from the coach, along with a sum of money. The theory is that it's "people from outside": people who don't live in Laborde. Here, like everywhere, blame is assigned to the others, the outsiders, the strangers. Then, in the car, neither Rodolfo, nor Miriam, nor Fernando says a word, and it feels to me as though I'm transporting someone to the gallows, and we're taking the long way round.

We find a parking spot on a dirt track alongside the grounds. When we get there the delegation from Chile is up on stage. It's still early, but we head to the changing rooms regardless. Rodolfo goes into number 2. Then, like a recurring dream, the whole thing repeats: water bottle, sash and *rastra* from the plastic bag, normal clothes off, wetting the hair, the caged-animal movements. Then the Bible, the whispered reading from it, shutting it and kissing it, placing it back in the bag. The phone, and pressing play on 'I Know You' by Almafuerte.

It's half-past midnight.

How many times can a man go through this?

How many times can I go through it?

Could this turn out to be a story that doesn't have an end?

———————

THE PLACE IS PACKED. The Argentinian flag ripples high above. Rodolfo is in his changing room, sitting on a chair and staring at the floor. Miriam goes over to him, hugs him, and, without a word, leaves. A little way off, Sebastián Sayago, dressed in the *norteño* attire, is standing in front of the mirror saying to himself:

"Let's go, let's go, let's go." At two o'clock the Laborde anthem strikes up and, as it finishes, the fireworks go off. Over the sound of the fireworks comes the voice of the announcer:

"Ladies and gentlemen, Laborde, the nation! Now is the moment of truth, the one you've all been waiting for! This is the reason they're here! Only one of them can be champion! Ladies and gentlemen... the Senior Soloists! It's time to get started, the final round!" After a breath, she says: "Representing La Pampa... Rodolfo... González... Alcántara!"

And out he goes.

———

THE DEADPAN VOICE:

"Time used: four minutes and forty-nine seconds."

Rodolfo exits the stage. His toes are covered in blood, there are grazes on the knuckles, and one of his feet has taken a gash. A journalist leaps forward for an interview while, on stage, it's Sebastián Sayago's turn. It's 2.20 a.m. Now the only thing left to do is wait.

Rodolfo puts on a jacket – he's bathed in sweat and the night is cold – and heads out to say hello to his family. Only subsequently do I find out that not all of them were able to watch, because they didn't have the money to pay the entry fee.

———————

AT FOUR O'CLOCK Rodolfo asks his brother-in-law Javier to get him an *alfajor* – a *dulce de leche*-based biscuit – as it's been a year and a half since he's eaten one. At 4.15 a.m. he needs to pee, which means removing some of his costume so he can go. At 4.30 a.m. he comes back, gets dressed again, sits in the changing room doorway and, with his jacket draped over his shoulders, eats the two *alfajors* that Javier bought. The Río Negro entrant has shut himself inside his changing room, Sebastián Sayago in his. Miriam is making plans via her phone so that she can be well positioned for the prize-giving ceremony. Tonchi is curled up beneath the cement table, contemplating the world as though very afraid. Rodolfo finishes his *alfajors* and goes inside. He sits down in a chair and I go over and sit facing him on an upturned beer crate. I notice he's holding a Sacred Heart icon in his right hand – I don't know where he got it. Tonchi cracks jokes – he reminds Rodolfo of a time when they were young and didn't want to sleep their siesta. Rodolfo nods, chuckles, does his best to say something.

"Nervous?" I ask him, after a short while.

Rodolfo nods at me – making sure that Tonchi doesn't see.

AT FIVE O'CLOCK people in the audience have covered themselves with blankets against the dawn chill. But inside the changing room Rodolfo is perspiring. The start of the prize-giving ceremony has been announced, and all representatives from all the delegations have been asked to come on stage. The ceremony is slow because third, second and first from each of the categories are handed out individually, sometimes including a few words for the dancer in question. At 5.15 a.m. it's begun to get light. And then at 5.30 a.m.:

"And now, ladies and gentlemen, the Senior Soloist category!"

Rodolfo, sitting in the corner, says nothing. Tonchi, beneath the cement table, says nothing. And I, sitting on the plastic crate, say nothing either.

"First of all we'll give you this year's runner-up. Ladies and gentlemen, this year's runner-up, the runner-up of this, the forty-fifth year of the most Argentinian of all festivals, hails from..." The announcer takes a breath, and, on the exhalation, says: "from Santiago del Estero! It's Sebastián Sayago!"

I glance outside the changing room. Sebastián emerges and Sayago makes his way to the stage. He doesn't look happy, and a good number of the people with him are in tears. Another year, I say to myself. Another year of twelve malambos every day, an hour's run. Another year of dreaded hope.

Rodolfo gets to his feet and, with the Sacred Heart icon in his hand, turns away from me and starts to pray.

The announcer invites Gonzalo Molina, El Pony, to go and dance his final malambo. El Pony dances – a dance I do not see – and when he has finished takes the microphone and begins speaking of his friends, his family, of his eternal gratitude. His words are muffled by the emotion, as well as the fact he doesn't stand close enough to the microphone.

Rodolfo finishes saying his prayers, places his hat on his head and exits the changing room. Miriam, Carlos Medina and Fernando Castro are waiting outside: their faces all look as though they have survived some tragedy, or as though they are expecting a catastrophe. As though Rodolfo were made of overly fragile material, no one goes over to him, no one says anything to him. Then we hear the announcer's voice:

"Ladies and gentlemen... Now, the name you have all been waiting to hear, the name of this year's champion!"

Rodolfo is pacing around. Miriam, leaning against a wall, watches him – she looks as though she would like to shriek something at him, or to cry. Tonchi leans out of the changing room door.

"The jury has this year named as National Malambo Champion..."

Then the name of the champion explodes from the microphone, and the following is the first thing to happen: Tonchi and Rodolfo embrace and fall to their knees. Tonchi bursts out crying while Rodolfo, holding onto Tonchi, does not; he screws his eyes shut, as though he's just been struck. Fireworks are going off outside, and the world revolves around these two men now, this small nucleus of unconditional friendship, pulsing with all the hungry winters, Tonchi's faulty kidneys, old trainers belonging to Rodolfo – because the announcer has just said that the new champion of Laborde, ladies and gentlemen, is him, is Rodolfo González Alcántara, and Miriam claps her hands over her mouth and weeps, Carlos Medina weeps, Fernando Castro weeps and Rodolfo and Tonchi remain where they are, down on their knees, until Miriam goes over, and Rodolfo gets up and they share a hug, and then Fernando Castro too, and then the Laborde anthem begins to play.

"Where's the champion?" the announcer is saying. "Where's the champion?"

Carlos Medina, drying his eyes, says:

"Rodo, Rodo, you've got to go out on stage!"

Rodolfo runs his hand through his hair, positions the hat on his head and goes out. And the first thing he does, before being handed the trophy by El Pony, is to embrace the runner-up, Sebastián Sayago.

THERE HE IS, I say.

There stands a man whose life is irrevocably changed.

No more sliding under the turnstiles in the metro.

No more trainers with worn-out soles.

No more hunger.

EL PONY HANDS OVER the trophy and Rodolfo lifts it above his head, places it down on the stage, then raises his hands and crosses himself. The announcer says:

"What a wonderful dedication, and barely 5.30 in the morning! Now it's time for a dance from the 2012 National Malambo Champion, Rodolfo González Alcántara!"

And, as is traditional, Rodolfo dances a few of the figures of the first malambo of his life as champion, and what will be one of the last malambos of his life. Following that, he goes to the microphone and, in an unwavering voice, making no concessions whatsoever to the tears, says:

"Hello. What I would like to do is to thank people. My family, because what they've done is incredible. Since they couldn't afford to camp, in order to be here they rented a 45-seater coach, which was cheaper, and when they go home they're going to have to all work really hard to pay the money back. All my tutors, thank you. To all the friends I've made along the way. To my wife, Miriam. Because we, the malambistas, put a lot of effort in, but the ones who make the sacrifice are those who are there beside us. So thank you all."

It's quarter to six in the morning of the first day of the rest of his life.

ONE YEAR ON, Saturday, 12th January 2013, the first
thing I see upon entering Laborde is a giant photo of
Rodolfo. Then, turning the corner, another. Followed
by another and another. His feet and hands, his waist,
half his body, his whole body – they've been dispersed
across the town like some crazed act of cannibalism. It's
six o'clock in the evening and, inside the grounds, an
open Q&A session in the press room between the champion and members of the public is coming to a close. In
sweater and jeans (cuffs rolled up), Rodolfo is signing
a series of small posters, pictures of himself. Each one
takes him a long time: he asks who it's for, the exact
spelling of the name, and then always writes a lengthy
dedication. He's told me that he has been having trouble
sleeping, and that he doesn't want to think about the
final malambo he's due to dance on Monday.

Walking through Laborde with him is impossible:
an entire football team, out for a jog, call out to him:
"Rodolfo González Alcántara! Stud!" There are people
asking for photos, autographs, a hug. He smiles, greets
people, is patient, personable, and modest; when the
owner of the Riccione ice cream parlour calls to ask if
he'll come by, because she has a giant print she wants
to give him as a present, Rodolfo, who's in his gaucho

get-up, asks me to come with him because he feels silly walking around like this outside the dance grounds.

His life altered vastly in 2012. Not only does he have more work – as a jury member at other festivals, as a teacher – his fees have gone up considerably. Using a quantity of money he never thought he'd have, he built a dance space in the house in Pablo Podestá for classes. In the future there's a good chance he'll be able to give up the classes in the other parts of the city and concentrate solely on teaching at the IUNA and at home.

Later, coming up to eight o'clock in the evening, the sky is still light and we're in the car, parked on a dirt track across from the cemetery. We can see a soya field that last year was corn. Has he carried on training, I ask?

"Yes," he says, "I went dune scrambling the last time I was in Santa Rosa. But it's hard without a goal. When I was training for Laborde, I always thought there was another dancer, at the same time, somewhere out there in the country, practising their malambo ten times a day. So I'd do mine twelve times. Or that there was someone running an hour a day – so I'd run an hour and a half. If you don't have a reason, it's hard to keep up that sort of rhythm."

"And was it what you expected, winning?"

"Much more. They idolize you. This last week here, I've felt like a king. I know that I'll never feel like I have this week in Laborde, never again in my life. But come Monday, all the attention is going to shift onto someone else."

We've come to the grounds early this evening because Rodolfo's student, Álvaro Melián, is dancing at 9.30 p.m. in the Advanced Teen category. Rodolfo says that if Álvaro were to win in his category, and Sebastián Sayago were to be champion, that would be his perfect outcome. Though people are saying Sebastián danced well this year, there's also the thought that he never recovered from the injury he had in 2012; if he makes the final, he'll have to dance through considerable pain.

"If the championship ended with those two things," says Rodolfo as we make our way to the changing room area, "it would be a dream. Sebas deserves it. He's a very low-key guy, very humble. And I want him to win, with all my heart."

The changing room area has been painted white this year, and signs with black lettering announce Changing Room 1, Changing Room 2. A little girl dressed in *paisana* regalia asks for an autograph, and Rodolfo asks if she minds waiting because his pupil is about to go on.

"Sure," she says. "It isn't as if you ever stop being champion, anyway."

Rodolfo smiles and touches her head. Taking up a position in the wings, as Álvaro begins his dance, I see

Rodolfo do what I've seen him do so many times before: make the sign of the cross.

_____

AT TWO O'CLOCK on Sunday afternoon the Senior Soloist finalists are announced: Rodrigo Heredia, for Córdoba; Ariel Pérez, for Buenos Aires; and Sebastián Sayago, for Santiago del Estero. Rodolfo's student Álvaro has also made it to the final in his category.

At three o'clock on Monday morning, Rodolfo is in the press room wearing his *norteño* costume. His nostrils are plugged with pieces of toilet roll.

"I think it's because I slept with the air conditioning on," he says.

He's been on stage several times since Tuesday, dancing a *zamba*, a *vals*, a *cueca*. Active participation the year after a champion wins is an important part of the agreement; as well as a number of exchange trips to Chile, Bolivia and Paraguay, champions also give a malambo workshop in Laborde – all unpaid.

The Senior Soloist finalists have danced. In spite of his injury, Sebastián Sayago danced a rousing *norteño*; opulent, dramatic – a devastating performance. Fernando

Castro, looking on from the foot of the stage, had tears streaming down his face by the end.

"He did what he had to," says Rodolfo. "It was totally emphatic. But now for the wait."

Miriam is talking with her parents, who have travelled up from Patagonia. Fernando Castro, who has moved and is now teaching traditional dance in a northern city called Salta, dressed impeccably in jeans and shirt, is tuning his guitar. Rodolfo puts some drops in his nose, poses for a photo with Laborde's female mayor. At this time last year, I think, Tonchi was curled up beneath the table in changing room 2, apparently expecting a devastating gale to blow in, and Rodolfo was adding to his nerves by praying to an icon.

At four o'clock in the morning, Rodolfo dons the *sureño* outfit and runs through his malambo in the mirror.

At 4.30 a.m. we head to the stage.

THE PRIZE-GIVING CEREMONY is, once again, lengthy. At 5.30 in the morning we know that Álvaro Melián has not won his category and that the Senior

Soloist runner-up is Ariel Pérez of Buenos Aires. Then comes the announcement that it's time to bid farewell to the 2012 champion.

"The nation is together here in the capital of malambo, and on we go through this rollercoaster of a final! It's the forty-sixth final! Now we have La Pampa's Rodolfo González Alcántara, the champion of 2012! The whole nation has shown him how much it loves him, all year long! And a champion bids farewell by dancing, here for you in the most Argentinian of all festivals!"

Rodolfo crosses himself in the wings and goes out. "Come on, Rodo!" come the cries. "Go, Champion!"

It's 5.45 a.m.

And it's thirty seconds short of 5.50 a.m. when he completes the final step of the last malambo of his life, and the applause comes raining down. He kisses the boards, gets to his feet and approaches the microphone.

"This is a difficult place to be. I didn't want that dance to end – though my body isn't up to it now! I woke up this morning feeling pretty low – I wanted to weep because this is the end of my career. Laborde has given me everything, and today it takes everything. It all stays here. I hope to represent Laborde to the rest of the country, the best that I can. For those yet to come. For those who dream. Thank you all, people of Laborde, for making me feel like a king. For having given me so much. For having helped me be what I am."

People call out. Rodolfo holds his hands up in thanks. Then he steps away from the microphone and goes over to the side of the stage.

"Ladies and gentlemen," says the announcer. "Now to present to you the new National Malambo Champion..."

The sky is beginning to grow light, shot with the remnants of a few red clouds. The tension among the audience builds – a marble-like tension.

"Now Laborde speaks the champion's name – and Argentina and the whole world listens! Our forty-sixth champion! Ladies and gentlemen! The 2013 National Malambo Champion, from Santia—"

And before she has finished saying Santiago del Estero, before the words Sebastián Sayago can be spoken, the crowd erupts. Backstage, under a flurry of embraces, Sebastián is sobbing. From the far side of the stage Rodolfo looks at me, smiles, pumps a fist. Without thinking, I respond in kind. Sebastián goes up, embraces Rodolfo, receives the trophy and, while he dances his first malambo as champion – one of the final malambos of his life – Rodolfo slips away into the wings. Miriam is waiting there for him. His feet are bleeding and he hugs her. She cries, but he says nothing. A small boy comes over and taps him on the back.

"Can I have your autograph, Champion?"

Rodolfo extracts himself from the embrace and looks at the boy. He must be eight years old and, like all malambistas, he wears his hair long.

"Ay, little man. Of course. Where shall I write it?"

"My shirt," the boy says, indicating his back.

Crouching down, Rodolfo writes one of his careful dedications on the boy's back. Then, taking his leave with a kiss, he heads over to the press room and begins undressing in a corner. He removes the jacket, the *rastra*, the sash and the shirt. And, before putting them away into the brown plastic bag, he lays a kiss on each of them.

I didn't see him cry, but he was crying.

Acknowledgements

Cecilia Lorenc Valcarce, for all your help.

Translator's Acknowledgements

The translator would like to thank the author and Ana Sánchez Resalt, for their help and advice in preparing this book.

Pushkin Press was founded in 1997, and publishes novels, essays, memoirs, children's books—everything from timeless classics to the urgent and contemporary.

Our books represent exciting, high-quality writing from around the world: we publish some of the twentieth century's most widely acclaimed, brilliant authors such as Stefan Zweig, Marcel Aymé, Antal Szerb, Gaito Gazdanov and Yasushi Inoue, as well as compelling and award-winning contemporary writers, including Andrés Neuman, Edith Pearlman, Erwin Mortier and Ayelet Gundar-Goshen.

Pushkin Press publishes the world's best stories, to be read and read again. Here are just some of the titles from our long and varied list. For more amazing stories, visit www.pushkinpress.com.

═══

THE SPECTRE OF ALEXANDER WOLF
GAITO GAZDANOV
'A mesmerising work of literature' Antony Beevor

BINOCULAR VISION
EDITH PEARLMAN
'A genius of the short story' Mark Lawson, *Guardian*

IN THE BEGINNING WAS THE SEA
TOMÁS GONZÁLEZ
'Smoothly intriguing narrative, with its touches of sinister, Patricia Highsmith-like menace' *Irish Times*

BEWARE OF PITY
STEFAN ZWEIG
'Zweig's fictional masterpiece' *Guardian*

THE PARROTS
FILIPPO BOLOGNA

'A five-star satire on literary vanity… a wonderful, surprising novel' *Metro*

SONG FOR AN APPROACHING STORM
PETER FRÖBERG IDLING

'Beautifully evocative… a must-read novel' *Daily Mail*

THE RABBIT BACK LITERATURE SOCIETY
PASI ILMARI JÄÄSKELÄINEN

'Wonderfully knotty… a very grown-up fantasy masquerading as
quirky fable. Unexpected, thrilling and absurd' *Sunday Telegraph*

STAMMERED SONGBOOK: A MOTHER'S BOOK OF HOURS
ERWIN MORTIER

'Mortier has a poet's eye for vibrant detail and prose to match… If this
is a book of fragmentation, it is also a son's moving tribute' *Observer*

THE BRETHREN
ROBERT MERLE

'Swashbuckling historical fiction… For all its philosophical depth
[*The Brethren*] is a hugely entertaining romp' *Guardian*

BARCELONA SHADOWS
MARC PASTOR

'As gruesome as it is gripping… the writing is extraordinar-
ily vivid… Highly recommended' *Independent*

THE LIBRARIAN
MIKHAIL ELIZAROV

'A romping good tale… Pretty sensational' *Big Issue*

WHILE THE GODS WERE SLEEPING
ERWIN MORTIER

'A monumental, phenomenal book' *De Morgen*

BUTTERFLIES IN NOVEMBER
·AUÐUR AVA ÓLAFSDÓTTIR

'A funny, moving and occasionally bizarre exploration of
life's upheavals and reversals' *Financial Times*

BY BLOOD

ELLEN ULLMAN

'Delicious and intriguing' *Daily Telegraph*

THE LAST DAYS

LAURENT SEKSIK

'Mesmerising… Seksik's portrait of Zweig's final months
is dignified and tender' *Financial Times*

TALKING TO OURSELVES

ANDRÉS NEUMAN

'This is writing of a quality rarely encountered… when you read Neuman's
beautiful novel, you realise a very high bar has been set' *Guardian*

JOURNEY INTO THE PAST

STEFAN ZWEIG

'Lucid, tender, powerful and compelling' *Independent*

FROM THE FATHERLAND, WITH LOVE

RYU MURAKAMI

'If Haruki is The Beatles of Japanese literature,
Ryu is its Rolling Stones' David Pilling

THE BREAK

PIETRO GROSSI

'Small and perfectly formed… reaching its end leaves the
reader desirous to start all over again' *Independent*

COIN LOCKER BABIES

RYU MURAKAMI

'A fascinating peek into the weirdness of contemporary Japan' Oliver Stone

CLOSE TO THE MACHINE

ELLEN ULLMAN

'Astonishing… impossible to put down' *San Francisco Chronicle*

MARCEL

ERWIN MORTIER

'Aspiring novelists will be hard pressed to achieve this quality' *Time Out*